# Radical Faith

RANDY McKEAN

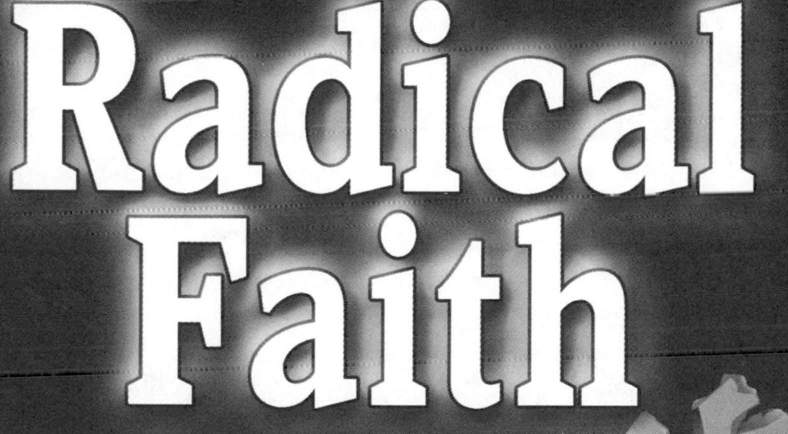


10 Faith Secrets

that will make faith in God work personally, powerfully and persistently!

**Radical Faith—10 Faith Secrets**



Printed in the United States of America.

ISBN: 978-1-941988-06-0.



Cover and interior book design: Toney Mulhollan. The text face is set in Maiola and Myriad Pro.

Copy Editor: Amy Morgan.

Illumination Publishers is committed to caring wisely for God's creation and uses recycled paper whenever possible.

**About the author:** Randy McKean was baptized into Christ in 1973 as a student at the University of Florida. He graduated with high honors with a degree in English, Religion and Education. He has served in the full-time ministry for thirty-five years in such diverse locations as Columbia, South Carolina; Tokyo, Japan; Munich, Germany; Paris, France and Boston, Massachusetts. While leading in Boston from 1990 to 2003, he simultaneously prepared and led mission teams to Europe. Currently Randy is serving with the Northern Virginia Church of Christ as both lead evangelist and as an elder. Randy has been married for thirty-eight years to his wife, Kay. They have two married children and four grandchildren.

www.ipibooks.com
6010 Pinecreek Ridge Court
Spring, Texas 77379-2513

# CONTENTS

# DEDICATION

*To my beautiful wife of thirty-eight years, Kay, who has made my life a dream come true. To my children, Summer and Kent, who have been two of the greatest joys in my life. To Paul and Heather, the best son-in-law and daughter-in-law a man could ever hope for. And to my grandkids—Ethan, Cadence, Savannah and Eden—the four wonders of my world!*

## PREFACE

# Shall We Hope or Shall We Die?

We all ask ourselves the "big" questions of life. Does God exist? How did the universe come into being? What is truth? Who is Jesus? Where did I come from? Is there life after death? And on we could go with these types of questions. For me, after looking at the mountains of evidence and reading the Bible for myself, I chose to have faith in God as he is revealed in the Bible, faith in Jesus as the Savior of the world and faith in the Bible as the word of God.

This is not an evidence book. It does not deal with Bible-based proofs or science-based proofs. There are many great books that do that. Neither is this book trying to give a treatise on the Bible's awesome doctrine of faith. There are many great books that do that also. This book is more unique. It is for those who already have faith in God, in Jesus and in the Bible and who need to more fully understand what this wonderful thing called faith is and how it can work in their lives. For so many, the concept of faith remains ethereal and confusing. For instance, many who sincerely want more faith know little more to do than to go to God in prayer again and again with the plea, "Give me more faith!... Give me more faith!... Give me more faith!" In the end, this becomes just an exercise in spiritual frustration. Instead, this book will give you an understanding of faith in concrete and practical ways.

Confusion is not a good thing. We all need explanations telling us the "who," "what," "where," "how" and "why." For example, there were times when Einstein would discreetly enter and attend a math or physics lecture. He would look around and see all the confusion on the faces of the students and note that the professors tended to explain things in ways that were hard to understand. He felt that they did this to look and feel superior. After the professors had finished their explanations, Einstein would raise his hand, go up to the board, put it all in plain language and then ask, "Is this what you mean? Do I have it right?" This, of course, would erase all the confusion and all the fuzziness in the students' minds. They would leave quite happy. I am no Einstein, but I do believe that after you read this book, you too will leave quite happy!

In this book, I will share with you faith secrets, or faith principles, into which God has given me insight as he has helped me to discover them in the Bible. Some of the things you will learn are how to know your potential for faith, how to measure your faith, how to increase your faith and how to use the power of faith. These principles or secrets are what I have built my life and my ministries on and they are the reason why God has caused so many amazing victories to occur in my life. They have allowed me to make my faith in God work personally, powerfully and persistently. I know they can do the same for you in your life. The results promise to be RADICAL!

Below are the lyrics for a song I wrote a number of years ago. It was actually written for a television show of the same name. It seemed appropriate to start a book about faith with it. It asks one main question...Shall We Hope or Shall We Die? I know what my answer is!

## SHALL WE HOPE OR SHALL WE DIE?

Randy McKean

Why do I live; is there a purpose for my being?
Is there something more to life than what I'm hearing, what I'm seeing?
Where do I go to find the truth I want and need?
Is man's philosophy the truth, or is there another book to read?

Shall we hope or shall we die?
I'm praying in the night;
Can't sleep without an answer;
Crying out to know what's right.
Shall we hope or shall we die?
The answer haunts my thinking.
We've been trying for so long;
Are we climbing now or sinking?
Shall we hope or shall we die?

Is there a God; is there a creator to be found?
Is my intellect misguided by the evidence around?
Is there hope; is there something to believe in?

Or should I live to simply die; are the promises deceiving?

Shall we hope or shall we die?
I'm praying in the night;
Can't sleep without an answer;
Crying out to know what's right.
Shall we hope or shall we die?
The answer haunts my thinking.
We've been trying for so long;
Are we climbing now or sinking?
Shall we hope or shall we die?

**rad-i-cal** *adj* 3a: marked by a considerable departure from the usual or traditional: EXTREME b: tending or disposed to make extreme changes in existing views, habits, conditions or institutions.

— *Merriam Webster's Collegiate Dictionary, Tenth Edition*

# PART ONE

# RADICAL FAITH

Success or failure...which would you choose? The truth is, no one walks around saying things like: "My goal in life is to be the biggest failure I can be" or "I love being a failure" or "Let me tell you about my latest failure." Failure is a scary word, a scary thought, a scary concept. Being a failure is not where we want to go in life! We all tend to shy away from anything that might lead us in the direction of failure; if it smells like failure, we go the opposite way.

What we all like is the smell of success. Success is the word we want to have describing our lives. And it's only a true faith in God that will give us true success. They go hand in hand. The "10 Faith Secrets" found later in this book will ensure a successful life...success being defined as victoriously living the life we were created to live. I call this the life of RADICAL FAITH.

When I was in fifth grade, I failed spelling. So I started cheating and got an A. I remember my teacher standing up in front of the class and announcing, "I believe someone in the class is cheating." That scared me, so you know what I started to do? I started to study! And you know what I got on those spelling tests? I started to get an A all the time. What an amazing thing! I learned there's the wrong way and the right way to experience success. RADICAL FAITH assures success in life the right way! *Everyone needs to learn it.*

I went to college at the University of Florida and became a Christian at the age of seventeen. With my school work, I was now striving to please God so I worked harder than ever. I got an A in all my classes except for one B in physical education—a basic gym class. At the end of the quarter I had been given a test in that class where I was to label parts of the heart and parts of the body. My thinking was, "Who couldn't get an A in a gym class?" so I didn't study too much for it. I had never been late for class, never missed a class and fully participated in every class...so no problem getting an A, right? But that turned out to be some bad thinking, as I found out (afterward) that whatever grade I made on the test would be the grade for the quarter. There's a bad way to think and a good way to think if we are to have success and live the life of RADICAL FAITH! *Everyone needs to learn it.*

A few years later, I had a required biology lab where I had to dissect a fetal pig. Fun stuff! I didn't like it at all. And since it was just a one-hour credit and all I needed was a C to pass, I didn't focus on it. I ended up with a D. Good news—there was a one-time forgiveness policy at the University of Florida. I retook the class, got an A and had the other grade "forgiven"...removed from my record. Nice! The better news is that God has an all-the-time forgiveness policy. Our success only comes from God's forgiveness. There's a way to live forgiven and live the life of RADICAL FAITH! *Everyone needs to learn it.*

Have you ever failed at love? I have. It doesn't feel very good. Actually, it feels really bad. The hurt can make a person pull back in some very wrong ways. I remember that first girl I thought I was in love with and thinking that our love would last forever. She lived two doors down from me when I was a junior in high school and she was a freshman. We dated for a number of months; I was enjoying all those wonderful feelings of infatuation and young love, when she said we needed to talk. Yes. She said it. "Let's just be friends." I was in pain and depressed. I listened to the latest sad love songs over and over and over again. After that I said to myself that I would do the breaking up from then on and would never get hurt like that ever again. Sound familiar? I lived in a very guarded way for a number of years. After becoming a Christian I started dating in a very new kind of way. In my sophomore year I found Kay—I should say that

God found Kay for me, because she has been both the wife I wanted and the wife I needed. We dated for a few months and then I desired to tell her how much I was in love with her. But this scared me. After all, what was her response going to be? I played out several different scenarios in my head. Maybe I would say, "Kay, I love you" and she would say nothing at all. Or maybe she would respond with, "I love you too...as a friend" or even worse, what if she just said, "Thanks"? Here's the rest of the story: when I said, "I love you," she said, "I love you too and I've wanted to tell you this for some time now." Why didn't I tell her earlier? Just fear. There was fear of the unknown and of getting hurt. Our success only comes with overcoming our fears. There's a way to live courageously and live the life of RADICAL FAITH! *Everyone needs to learn it.*

I have found that success is much better than failure. (You didn't need this book to tell you that, did you?) God created me for success—to victoriously live the kind of life I was created to live—to have marriage success and family success and work success. God wants me to enjoy life now and to live with him forever. But this life only comes together and holds together when we live a life of RADICAL FAITH. *Everyone needs to learn it.*

If the Bible had a subtitle, it would be *Radical Faith*. The things accomplished in the Bible are amazing. There are so many ordinary men and women of God who accomplish the extraordinary. That's the exciting, fulfilling and satisfying life God is calling us to. Doing things that have never been done before in our lives is what God is all about—and that's radical!

Faith in God is the door to success. This book will give you 10 Secrets of Radical Faith. These ten secrets are the key to unlock your door to success in the Christian life. Let's look at some scriptures about faith and how it moved ordinary people to do extraordinary things. Although these passages are probably familiar to most of you, try to read this as if it were your first time experiencing these words. Hebrews 11:1–39 (emphasis added) reads:

*Now **faith** is being sure of what we hope for and certain of what we do not see. This is what the ancients were commended for.*

*By **faith** we understand that the universe was formed at God's command, so that what is seen was not made out of what was visible.*

*By **faith** Abel offered God a better sacrifice than Cain did. By **faith** he was commended as a righteous man, when God spoke well of his offerings. And by **faith** he still speaks, even though he is dead.*

*By **faith** Enoch was taken from this life, so that he did not experience death; he could not be found, because God had taken him away. For before he was taken, he was commended as one who pleased God. And without **faith** it is impossible to please God, because anyone who comes to him must believe that he exists and that he rewards those who earnestly seek him.*

*By **faith** Noah, when warned about things not yet seen, in holy fear built an ark to save his family. By his **faith** he condemned the world and became heir of the righteousness that comes by **faith**.*

*By **faith** Abraham, when called to go to a place he would later receive as his inheritance, obeyed and went, even though he did not know where he was going. By **faith** he made his home in the promised land like a stranger in a foreign country; he lived in tents, as did Isaac and Jacob, who were heirs with him of the same promise. For he was looking forward to the city with foundations, whose architect and builder is God.*

*By **faith** Abraham, even though he was past age—and Sarah herself was barren—was enabled to become a father because he considered him faithful who had made the promise. And so from this one man, and he as good as dead, came descendants as numerous as the stars in the sky and as countless as the sand on the seashore.*

*All these people were still living by **faith** when they died. They did not receive the things promised; they only saw them and welcomed them from a distance. And they admitted that they were aliens and strangers on earth. People who say such things show that they are looking for a country of their own. If they had been thinking of the country they had left, they would have had opportunity to return. Instead, they were longing for a better country—a heavenly one. Therefore God is not ashamed to be called their God, for he has prepared a city for them.*

*By **faith** Abraham, when God tested him, offered Isaac as a sacrifice. He who had received the promises was about to sacrifice his one and only son, even though God had said to him, "It is through Isaac that your offspring will be reckoned." Abraham reasoned that God could raise the dead, and figuratively speaking, he did receive Isaac back from death.*

*By **faith** Isaac blessed Jacob and Esau in regard to their future.*

*By **faith** Jacob, when he was dying, blessed each of Joseph's sons, and worshiped as he leaned on the top of his staff.*

*By **faith** Joseph, when his end was near, spoke about the exodus of the Israelites from Egypt and gave instructions about his bones.*

*By **faith** Moses' parents hid him for three months after he was born, because they saw he was no ordinary child, and they were not afraid of the king's edict.*

*By **faith** Moses, when he had grown up, refused to be known as the son of Pharaoh's daughter. He chose to be mistreated along with the people of God rather than to enjoy the pleasures of sin for a short time. He regarded disgrace for the sake of Christ as of greater value than the treasures of Egypt, because he was looking ahead to his reward. By **faith** he left Egypt, not fearing the king's anger; he persevered because he saw him who is invisible. By **faith** he kept the Passover and the sprinkling of blood, so that the destroyer of the firstborn would not touch the firstborn of Israel.*

*By **faith** the people passed through the Red Sea as on dry land; but when the Egyptians tried to do so, they were drowned.*

*By **faith** the walls of Jericho fell, after the people had marched around them for seven days.*

*By **faith** the prostitute Rahab, because she welcomed the spies, was not killed with those who were disobedient.*

*And what more shall I say? I do not have time to tell about Gideon, Barak, Samson, Jephthah, David, Samuel and the prophets, who through faith conquered kingdoms, administered justice, and gained what was promised; who shut the mouths of lions, quenched the fury of the flames, and escaped the edge of the sword; whose weakness was turned to strength; and who became powerful in battle and routed foreign armies. Women received back their dead, raised to life again. Others were tortured and refused to be released, so that they might gain a better resurrection. Some faced jeers and flogging, while still others were chained and put in prison. They were stoned; they were sawed in two; they were put to death by the sword. They went about in sheepskins and goatskins, destitute, persecuted and mistreated—the world was not worthy of them. They wandered in deserts and mountains, and in caves and holes in the ground.*

*These were all commended for their **faith**.*

These are men and women who lived lives of radical faith. Now think about Jesus. When you read about his life in the gospels, all you can say is, "That's RADICAL!" You look at the book of Acts, the story of the early church and the evangelization of the known world and all you can say is, "That's RADICAL!" What would the story of your life be entitled? I can tell you the title that God wants you to adopt. He wants to look at your life and say, "That's RADICAL!" Christians are to be ever growing—always becoming more and more like Jesus Christ. Christians are to change from one degree of glory to another. This is the life that God has called us to. I use the title, *Radical Faith*, because it's an awesome description of the Christian life. After all, true faith is always radical. Saying "radical faith" is like saying "fiery sun." The sun is always fiery and true faith is *always* radical!

When I was baptized into Christ as a freshman in college, I made the decision that Jesus was going to be the Lord of my life for all of my life. I knew that I was turning away from sin and turning to God. I was committing to live my life as God wanted me to live it, as revealed in the Bible. This commitment was not just for a week, not just for a month, not just for a year, not just for the hard times and not just for the good times. I made a lifetime commitment that Jesus would be the Lord of my whole life. I remember it was about 11 pm on a Monday night. There were only a few other people there. I was baptized, had a prayer and then walked home to my dorm room. I was excited; I was feeling happy. My sins were now forgiven. I was really a Christian. My sins were washed away; I was finally right with God.

So I was feeling good—and then "real" life hit! After I became a Christian I was different. I was not alone, as the Holy Spirit now lived in me and empowered me, but still the new life hit me hard in the real world. There were so many new ways of thinking and living that God was calling me to. It was all new and it was all wonderful but...this new life was RADICAL for me! That, of course, is what makes it both challenging and thrilling.

Sharing my faith—that was radical. Studying the Bible with people to teach them about Christ—that was radical. Developing relationships with other Christians to get help and to give help (discipling)—that was radical. Leading small group Bible studies, speaking in front of large crowds and building friendships with people who were very different from me in culture and background was all radical. Learning how to fellowship, memorizing Scripture, having daily quiet times, leading public prayers, helping the poor and needy, sharing at communion, preaching (I feel sorry for those who were first listening!)—all of this and so much more was RADICAL for me.

A good example of a radical difference was with pure dating. That was a new way of life for me and for Kay (my wife now of thirty-eight years). The world and the Bible have such different standards. My first date with Kay was on February 8, 1975 and we got married on June 3, 1977. We enjoyed a pure dating relationship during that whole time as we built our friendship and our love. It developed a foundation for a strong marriage and family. The point is that there is so much that's new in the new life. But God always gives us the power to do whatever he commands us to do. That's something to always remember! Certainly it's a learning process, a growing process, but God stays with us and we must stay with God. We are to live by radical faith.

My wife and I went into the full-time ministry right after my graduation and our marriage. We have since lived in Charleston, Illinois; Columbia, South Carolina; Tokyo, Japan; Boston, Massachusetts; Orlando, Florida; Munich, Germany and Paris, France; and we presently live in Northern Virginia. We have preached, made our home or visited in over fifty countries around the world. We have helped to start churches in twenty-seven different nations. I have not lived the life I once dreamed of, but I have lived a dream life as I have followed Christ's dream of living a life of radical faith. This life's journey has not only taken me around the world, it has taught me the 10 Faith Secrets that I will share with you in this book.

Before I do, let me list some simple principles for living the life of radical faith or, as I like to call it, the KNOW-NO LIST. This will help prepare us for all that will be discussed in the pages of the rest of this book.

## THE KNOW-NO LIST

1. **KNOW GOD:** Know God's mercy, love, truth, compassion, power, presence, perfection. Your perception of life comes out of your understanding of and emotional connection to who God is. If you are not emotionally connected, then you will become disconnected from consistently living the Christian life. For example, when you are emotionally connected to your spouse and kids, you naturally consider them. This allows much of your best thinking and planning to focus on them. You are not automatically connected to them just because you come home every day and share the same space. In the same way, you are not automatically connected to God just because you go to church. Going to church is essential, but there must be correct Bible knowledge about God and an emotional connection to him that goes wherever you go. Then, because of this internal connection from the heart, you will find ways to serve and please him. In the end, it's all about your life away from the crowds; it's when you are alone that defines who you really are and if you really ***know God!***

2. **NO LIMITS:** There are no limits to what you can do except the limits that you place upon yourself. Get that Bible open and look at the promises that God has made to you and to every Christian. Those promises are right and true because they are made and said by God. Therefore, there are ***no limits!***

3. **KNOW CHANGE IS GOOD:** Your life only gets better when you get better. This means change. It's a simple concept. We all understand it, yet we can shy away or run away from change. We can get worried or fearful. Is change challenging? Yes. But not to change is even more challenging because it's

so damaging. Without continual change into the likeness of Christ, a person ends up in a hopeless kind of life—a disappointing kind of life—a boring kind of life. ***Know change is good!***

4. **NO VICTIM MENTALITY:** You can make your life better or worse. You can choose to do God's will or you can choose not to. It is your choice; it is your life. Don't blame failure on your background. Don't blame it on the people around you. Don't blame failure on your circumstances. Yes, it's true that others may have it better than you in these areas but, in the end, who you are in life and what you do in life is up to you. It is each individual's choice and each individual's responsibility. So, no blame games. ***No victim mentality!***
5. **KNOW MISTAKES AREN'T BAD:** Anything worth doing is worth trying, even if we don't do it so well at the beginning. Practice makes us better. We are to put into practice our Christianity. I am reminded of the story of the man visiting New York City for the first time. He was excited as he was on his way to an exclusive concert at Carnegie Hall. As he jumped into a taxi, he realized that he was running a little late. Nervous that he would miss the beginning of the concert, he struck up a conversation with the driver and asked how to get to Carnegie Hall. The driver just turned around and with a big smile answered, "Mister, there's only one way to get to Carnegie Hall...with PRACTICE, BABY, PRACTICE!" We don't get better in anything in life unless we practice. So don't be afraid to make mistakes as you try something new and challenging. That's how we all learn. That's how we get better. That's how we become everything God calls us to be. ***Know mistakes aren't bad!***
6. **NO TO SIN:** We are to count ourselves dead to sin. When

a person is dead, he does not respond. Tickle a dead person and there is no laughter. Hit a dead person and there is no reaction. There is no response, because he is dead. There is to be no response when sin comes knocking at our door. We must keep saying ***no to sin!***

7. **KNOW COURAGE IS ESSENTIAL:** There is a quote that says: "To discover new continents, you must be willing to lose sight of the shore." You've got to let go and lose sight and travel on faith, believing that God will lead you and that he will take care of you. This takes courage. ***Know courage is essential!***

8. **NO RUTS:** A car can get in a rut in the snow or mud, and when it does, it's not going anywhere. It's just spinning its wheels. Living life like this is a bad way to go. You are exerting energy but going nowhere. We are supposed to be the people who have the power of God because we have the Spirit of God living inside us. We are always to be developing. If we have stopped and are going nowhere spiritually, then we need to look for another direction to go—a different door to open. Insanity can be defined as doing the same thing over and over again hoping for a different result. Do something different! God always has open doors for us to move through. Be willing to go through doors that were not your first choice. Hitting a closed door over and over again hurts after a while! God calls us to a life that is joyful, a life that is full of adventure and satisfaction. So always keep moving forward—***no ruts!***

9. **KNOW THE POWER OF DISCIPLING:** A good working definition of discipling is: a committed friendship with another Christian that keeps up an ongoing, open dialogue about all that is happening in each other's lives (good and

bad), with the goal of helping each other to become more like Christ. This is a part of God's plan. No person can "fix" another person. Only God can "fix" us—change us. But God uses people in the process. Discipling is putting into practice the one-another commandments in the Scriptures: love one another, pray for one another, encourage one another, confess your sins to one another, forgive one another, etc. We are to use the power of discipling to keep us growing in Christ. Every Christian is to ***know the power of discipling!***

10. **NO SACRIFICE—NO BLESSING**: Sacrifice shows the depth of a person's desire. We always sacrifice for what we really love and what we really want. If only the scraps and leftovers of our time, efforts and talents are given for our Christianity, you can be sure of this—where there are no great sacrifices, there can be no great blessings. Sacrifice shows our love for God and our faith in him. It says, "I have convictions!" If you just want to play at this thing called Christianity or if you just want to play it safe or stay comfortable, then you can't possibly understand the way of the cross. You can't be walking in the footsteps of Jesus without sacrifice. Blessings come as we truly walk with Christ. God wants to bless us. The angels are on tiptoes waiting to rejoice in our blessings. But we must be willing to live the sacrificial lives God calls us to. Remember...***no sacrifice—no blessing!***

11. **KNOW PROBLEMS ARE GOOD:** The problems we have are either sent by God, allowed by God or caused by ourselves. Yes, sometimes we bring the problems into our own lives through the consequences of our own sin. But God is always trying to teach us valuable lessons for success and victory in the Christian life. He promises in Romans 8:28 that, even when we are the cause of the problem, he is still working

for our good. (He did not say all things are good or that all things have good results!) The Bible says that problems ultimately produce good things in us if we keep or get back to the right spiritual perspective. So, deep in your inner being, ***know problems are good!***

12. **NO PERSEVERANCE—NO SUCCESS:** Successful Christian living comes to those who are willing to launch out after their goals day after day, week after week, month after month and year after year with perseverance. We are to continue to do the right thing even when there is every human reason to give up. Why? Because of our faith in God. ***No perseverance—no success!***

How does this sound to you? How about living life on the level that God calls us to? How about living a life of radical faith? What mark are you going to make for God with your life? What legacy are you going to leave your children and grandchildren? What difference are you going to make in the history of this world? Each person must wrestle with these questions. Each person must pray about them. Let us live the life God has called us to live. God guarantees success when we live it his way...living by *radical faith*.

There was a man named Sir Edmund Hillary. At first he failed in climbing Mt. Everest. Eventually, he was successful. Let's close Part 1 with his story.

> Sir Edmund Hillary was the first person to climb Mt. Everest, the tallest mountain in the world. He failed on his initial effort, but he had made a valiant effort and Parliament wanted to recognize him for it. They felt that he deserved the recognition. They put a picture of Mt. Everest on the wall of their chambers. They invited him in. They stood as one, a standing ovation for the good effort that Sir Edmund Hillary had made. As he walked to the front of the room to address Parliament, tears welled up in

> his eyes. They were not tears of happiness. They were not tears of joy. They were tears of anger and frustration. He had not set out to make a good effort to climb that mountain. He had not set out to leave five of his associates dead on the side of that mountain. He had set out to climb Mt. Everest. He was at a crossroads in his life. He knew that if he accepted the accolades for making a good effort that he would never climb that mountain. As he walked to the front of the room, he looked at the picture; he looked at those legislators standing and applauding for him. He recognized something that many of us never recognize. And that was this: yes, he had made a good effort, but the greatest enemy of excellence is good. He would not be satisfied with that good effort. He would only be satisfied by climbing that mountain. He walked to the front of the room. He looked again at that picture of Mt. Everest. He looked at those people standing there applauding. He literally walked over to that picture and he pounded on that inanimate object and he hollered at it and he screamed at it. And he said: "You defeated me once, but you will never defeat me again, because you have grown all that you can grow but I am still growing!" (author unknown)

He went back and climbed Mt. Everest! This beautifully illustrates the life God intends us to live. As you begin this book, cry out to God about the mountains that have defeated you, the mountains that you need to conquer. It may be the mountain of discipline, the mountain of materialism, or the mountain of prejudice. It may be the mountain of marriage challenges, the mountain of health issues, or the mountain of grief and loss. It may be the mountain of personal finances, the mountain of forgiveness, the mountain of child-raising issues or the mountain of addiction. It may be the mountain of pornography, of reconciliation, or of fear in sharing your faith. But whatever the mountains are in your life, decide right now to scale your mountains by living the life of RADICAL FAITH through embracing the 10 Faith Secrets in this book. Decide right now to cry out along with Sir Edmund Hillary...***"I AM STILL GROWING!"***

# PART TWO

# DEEP FAITH

RADICAL FAITH is DEEP FAITH. The fire of faith must burn *deep* within every disciple's heart. We are called to have and maintain a deep faith. There's a big difference between the question, "Are you fired up?" and the question, "Do you have fire in your heart?" This fire of faith can't be a feeling that's here today and gone tomorrow. It can't be something dependent on a person's circumstances; this fire of faith is to be ever burning deep within.

Do you have fire in your heart? Sometimes we speak our answers to important questions too quickly. I am reminded of the TV installation man who came to a certain house. After his being there for a few minutes, the homeowner said she was stepping out to go next door. When the front door closed, the TV installation man noticed a large, black Doberman coming into the same room where he was working. The dog growled, bared its teeth and then stopped about seven feet away and carefully watched. Since the dog came no closer, the man cautiously went on with his work. A few minutes later, a loud parrot that was in a cage in the corner of the room started talking incessantly. The bird kept repeating, "Hello. How are you? Polly wants a cracker... Hello. How are you? Polly wants a cracker... Hello. How are you? Polly wants a cracker." After fifteen minutes of this repetition, it really got on the installation man's nerves. Finally, he got angry and shouted, "You dumb bird, can't you say anything else?" The parrot cocked his head and loudly said, "Sic him!"

Yes, sometimes we speak too quickly! So make sure you think before you answer. The question is...do YOU have fire in your heart?

If we could break open the heart of a true Christian, what

would be found? Humility. Mercy. Compassion. Love. Joy. Purity. Peace...and FIRE!

> *"I have come to bring fire on the earth, and how I wish it were already kindled! But I have a baptism to undergo, and how distressed I am until it is completed!" (Luke 12:49–50)*

Jesus came to establish his kingdom on earth. Before he could do that, he had to be immersed (baptized) into pain, suffering and death. Then salvation could be available to mankind and the kingdom could begin.

God's kingdom of heaven on earth is the church. The church is made up of the forgiven people belonging to God. It is to be a fire that never gets extinguished. The nature of fire is to spread. The church is to spread like wildfire into all the world! Every single Christian is to be on fire for God. This is not for the few or even for the many who wear the name of Christ; being on fire for God is for *all* who call themselves a true follower of Jesus. And let's not forget the words of Jesus...that the kingdom of God is within. So, where must the fire be? It must be within!

> *Once, having been asked by the Pharisees when the kingdom of God would come, Jesus replied, "The kingdom of God does not come with your careful observation, nor will people say, 'Here it is,' or 'There it is,' because the kingdom of God is within you." (Luke 17:20–21)*

> *Do not put out the Spirit's fire. (1 Thessalonians 5:19)*

> *These are the words of the Amen, the faithful and true witness, the ruler of God's creation. I know your deeds, that you are neither cold nor hot. I wish you were either one or the other! So, because you are lukewarm — neither hot nor cold—I am about to spit you out of my mouth. (Revelation 3:14–16)*

What is going to keep the fire burning? Faith! It is the fuel for the fire. Faith starts the fire and keeps it burning. There must be deep faith living inside us.

We live in a world that lacks convictions. The convictions it does have are shallow and ever changing. The world says there are no absolutes except for one...that there are *absolutely* no absolutes! The world asks the questions, "What is politically correct?" or "What is acceptable?" or "What does the majority say?" But deep convictions take courage. It means you will stand up and stand firm. It means you will make a difference in this world. It means the people around you will know exactly who you are and what you are all about. It will be obvious. There are far too many who wear the name Christian but are only *masters of the oblique*...those who have mastered the art of almost saying something!

## Three Truths to Consider about Convictions

1. Your present convictions determine your present lifestyle!
2. The depth of your convictions determines the longevity of a changed life!
3. The correctness of your convictions determines your eternal destiny!

So, we had better get our convictions right and deep! When Paul came to Thessalonica to establish the church, the Bible says he came with deep conviction.

> *For we know, brothers and sisters loved by God, that he has chosen you, because our gospel came to you not simply with words but also with power, with the Holy Spirit and deep conviction. (1 Thessalonians 1:4–5)*

Deep conviction is just another way of saying deep faith. The deep faith in God that Paul and his companions had was transferred into the hearts of those who responded to the gospel message.

Before I was a Christian, I had convictions. These were not necessarily Bible convictions, but they were my beliefs, my faith, which

I built my life on. Some convictions were deep. Some were shallow. Some were right and some were wrong. One of my deep convictions was that I would not get drunk or do drugs. To this day, I have never been drunk and have never used illegal drugs. This doesn't make me better than anyone—it was just a life choice that happened to be a right one. This choice kept me out of some of the hurts and scars that come with these particular sins. Some of my shallow and, therefore, wavering convictions had to do with purity in the sexual realm. I told myself no premarital sex. Wait for the right one—the one for all your life. Wait for the wedding night! I had this conviction not because I necessarily loved God, although I did have some Bible knowledge on this subject. Much of my lifestyle was based on the kind of home I grew up in and the expectations that were there. As the time grew closer to move away from home, I was also moving away from my "environmental" convictions. I didn't say no to pornography when it came my way. I messed up with some impurity (petting) in my senior year of high school and would certainly have gotten into the sex scene in college if I had not become a Christian so early in my freshman year. And so, as I look back at this time in my life, I see that I had some deep convictions and some shallow convictions, some right convictions and some wrong convictions. I had not been taught the Bible well, so my convictions were more based on what I thought and felt instead of being based on what God thought and commanded.

In my first few months as a Christian, I learned a lot of Bible in a short period of time and so had many new convictions. What I didn't have was the time it takes to make new convictions deep. Knowing what is right and following it through are two very different things. For instance, there was a girl that I had feelings for before I became a Christian. Now trust me, I had many more feelings for her than she did for me! In going home from college for the first time after becoming a disciple, I knew the right thing was to talk to her and share my faith with her. I did this. She had no real interest;

therefore, I knew I had to deal with my feelings about her. So I did well with this one situation. Then I met another girl on that same Christmas break. We went out on a few dates, kissed and hugged, and I developed feelings for her. Can you believe this? I had done so well at first...but the depth of my convictions still needed developing. I went back to college, got back into the strong campus fellowship and never called or wrote this second girl. It was the coward's way out, but at least I ended up doing the right thing—having the conviction that real Christians date and marry only real Christians!

After being a disciple for about a year, I was not as deep with my personal relationship with God as I needed to be. Also, I hadn't developed the deep, honest relationships that are needed and commanded in the Christian life. I was very busy with all the church services and activities and was even leading an evangelistic Bible study, but I was feeling lonely. I was even thinking this love thing in the fellowship seemed superficial and unreal. I had changed a great amount in my actions, my thinking and my desires, but I was still very independent. I had a lot of pride and insecurity (a typical combination!) although I came across confident and strong. On top of that, there was some of that basic worldliness. I was attracted to what the world seemed to offer. During this time I thought about leaving God. Instead, I opened up about my feelings and thoughts. After that, it was amazing how real and loving everyone else became! Of course, all the Christians didn't change; it was I who changed. We tend to read into others' hearts what is really in our own. My heart and mind had been clouded by my old nature. I got back on track and learned some valuable spiritual lessons.

Now that I've been a Christian for forty-two years, the basic moral issues of life are not my main struggle. I find the greater battle is to keep my convictions deep and not to lose them in the day-to-day living of this busy, material world. I see this as the main battleground for older disciples. A loss of faith (which translates into a loss of keeping the right priorities) can enter the heart through hurt feelings, self-pity, resentments, bitterness, feelings of not being believed in, or feelings of being unappreciated. It can come with our disappointments in life. I've seen people retreat spiritually because they did not get what they wanted—the Christian life just didn't turn out for them the way they thought it would. I've heard people talk about not getting their dreams fulfilled and then becoming angry with God. I've seen people blame their problems in life on a leader, on a church or on the Christians around them. I've noticed some turn their back on God because of their sense of entitlement. They feel they have sacrificed such-and-such *for* God and so they deserve such-and-such *from* God. Others struggle or have doubts in their faith because of the death of a loved one or because of a personal health issue. All of these things, if not dealt with at the heart level with God, can erode and eventually destroy a person's faith, convictions and priorities. People can become disillusioned and disheartened. One important note here: leaving God is not always walking out of church and back into the old sins and the old patterns of life. Leaving God can also mean staying in church with a lukewarm commitment to the commands of God and a lukewarm appreciation of the love and grace of God. We must always protect our faith. We must always grow our faith. We must always deepen our faith.

I will share three of the challenging, emotional and defining times for my faith as an older Christian. After being a Christian for fourteen years, my wife and I decided to go on the mission field, believing this was the greatest need of the hour. To enable us to do this, we sacrificed a secure position, a house and our savings. Then after being promised a certain mission destination, it was changed without my knowledge to something else. I had placed my heart into the original plan of Tokyo and had already worked and sacrificed for it. My family and I had spent a summer in Tokyo developing the plans and developing the team. The way the changes were made did not feel good and was not "right" from my point of view. I felt that my dream had been taken away. At this point, I had to work on my heart. I had to do some deep soul-searching. I had to decide if I had the faith that God was at work even in the midst of some hurt and some unkept promises. I had to figure out if I was more in love with my dream or more in love with my God! After getting my heart right, my wife and I were able to have two life experiences that I would not change for the world. We planted a church in Munich, Germany and then went on to restart a congregation in Paris, France. This led to working with twenty-four different European nations over a time span of fifteen years. We saw many souls saved and many lives changed by the love of God. We made wonderful friends, and our children's faith in God was shaped and developed during these years as they witnessed all that God was doing.

Another challenge to my faith came after serving in the full-time ministry for twenty-seven years. During a period of ministry changes, I was asked to step down and step out from my ministry responsibilities. The publicly stated reason was that there was no money at the time for a missions evangelist. At this point, I was forty-seven years old physically and thirty years old spiritually. All I had ever done besides odd jobs in high school and college was to work in the ministry. It was a time of separation from the people I loved and from the work I had given so much of my life to build. I grieved over this loss. I felt thrown away. This certainly did not seem "fair" or "right." It was a hard transition time finding different work and building a different life. I had to remind myself that God had always taken care of me and he would continue to take care of me and my family. I eventually went to work on a sales team for a structural engineering firm for several years, and my wife worked at a hospital. After a period of time, I enjoyed making more money than I had ever made in the ministry, taking longer vacations, living in a nicer house than ever before, driving a better car, living in a warm climate close to family, and feeling much freedom in only working a forty- to forty-five-hour work week. During this time, my wife and I never gave up going to all the church services, reading our Bibles, giving our contribution or reaching out to the lost. It was a time of testing and a time of training. I certainly learned things I probably would not have learned any other way. I had to fight with myself and deal with my emotions so I would not lose or water down my convictions. It was not an easy time and not a desired time. I had not chosen it. But, in the end, it was a defining time for my faith.

Again a time of testing came for my faith when my wife said we should go back into the full-time ministry. I was now fifty-one years old and thirty-four years old as a Christian. I had gotten comfortable (not necessarily in a sinful way) with a new life in a new place. Also, at fifty-one years old, I was thinking a lot more about our financial situation and security for the future. Going back into the ministry would mean a cut in pay from what I had become used to earning. And then there was the issue of the size of the ministry job. I would be starting over in many ways—it certainly was a pride/humility issue for me. There was also the fact that I was very attached to my home. It was my dream home; I loved it and enjoyed it! Yet I knew within my heart that I wasn't as fulfilled; I knew that ministry was what I did best. God found us a ministry home with the Northern Virginia Church, and it has been amazing to see all that he has done in such a short period of time through the great-hearted disciples in the church. Keeping faith through all of life is certainly the big challenge!

> *These have come so that your faith—of greater worth than gold, which perishes even though refined by fire—may be proved genuine and may result in praise, glory and honor when Jesus Christ is revealed. (1 Peter 1:7)*

## Joshua

Joshua is such an awesome example of a man holding on to his faith. He delivered the faithful report about the Promised Land, but his report was ignored. He could have developed an attitude towards

God and towards leadership, as it was "unfair" for him to be wandering in the desert for all those years. And certainly, life had not turned out like Joshua thought it would. But he kept his faith strong through the years!

> *"I was forty years old when Moses the servant of the LORD sent me from Kadesh Barnea to explore the land. And I brought him back a report according to my convictions, but my brothers who went up with me made the hearts of the people melt with fear. I, however, followed the LORD my God wholeheartedly. . .*
>
> *"Now then, just as the LORD promised, he has kept me alive for forty-five years since the time he said this to Moses, while Israel moved about in the desert. So here I am today, eighty-five years old! I am still as strong today as the day Moses sent me out; I'm just as vigorous to go out to battle now as I was then." (Joshua 14:7–8, 10–11)*

## Jesus

The deep faith of Jesus is another great example and inspiration. He had to keep his convictions deep and real as he got closer and closer to his suffering and death. His resolve about going to the cross and attaining salvation for all mankind is a demonstration of his deep faith.

> *As the time approached for him to be taken up to heaven, Jesus resolutely set out for Jerusalem. (Luke 9:51)*

> *At that time some Pharisees came to Jesus and said to him, "Leave this place and go somewhere else. Herod wants to kill you."*
>
> *He replied, "Go tell that fox, 'I will drive out demons and heal people today and tomorrow, and on the third day I will reach my goal.' In any case, I must keep going today and tomorrow and the next day—for surely no prophet can die outside Jerusalem!" (Luke 13:31–33)*

## Judas and Peter

Deep faith is developed through time, through experiences, through persecutions, through challenges, through victories, through openness, through repentance, through joys, through sorrows, through blessings, through pain, through fear...and deep faith is also developed through defeats. Yes, there are defeats. Defeats don't come because of a lack of God's power; they come through our sin or through the sin of those around us. The big issue is how we handle life as we go through it. The determining factor is the development of the inside man or inside woman. The outside may look similar, but it is the development or lack of development of deep faith that causes one person to stand and another to fall.

Judas and Peter ended up having very different hearts although they went through similar experiences and had similar opportunities. Both heard the same teachings of Jesus and both saw the same miracles of Jesus. The difference was the depth of their convictions.

It seems like many have a misunderstanding of who Judas really was. This misunderstanding can even lead to feeling sorry for him as if he had no choice in his betrayal of Jesus. Judas was a talented, awesome, spiritual guy. When Jesus chose his twelve apostles, he didn't pick eleven great guys and one obvious dud! At the last supper when Jesus said one of the twelve would betray him, all heads didn't turn towards Judas, the dud, with a knowing look. Instead all were perplexed, and John even asked who it would be. There were incredible things all these men had done, had seen, had been a part of and had accomplished. But Judas had a hidden sin that he never dealt with: he loved money. God tells us that the love of money is a root for all kinds of evil and that some people who are eager for money will wander away from the faith and pierce themselves with many griefs (1 Timothy 6:10). Judas was the designated one who carried the money for the poor, and he used to steal from it. He was offered money for his betrayal and he took the deal. I doubt Judas ever thought his betrayal would lead to Jesus' death. But isn't this the way of sin? It has far greater consequences than we think. Below is how Judas handled all of this:

> *Early in the morning, all the chief priests and the elders of the people came to the decision to put Jesus to death. They bound him, led him away and handed him over to Pilate, the governor.*
>
> *When Judas, who had betrayed him, saw that Jesus was condemned, he was seized with remorse and returned the thirty silver coins to the chief priests and the elders. "I have sinned," he said, "for I have betrayed innocent blood."*
>
> *"What is that to us?" they replied. "That's your responsibility."*
>
> *So Judas threw the money into the temple and left. Then he went away and hanged himself. (Matthew 27:1–5)*

At first, it looks good. It looks like Judas is getting back on the right track and on the right team. He returned the money. That seems like awesome repentance. He was seized with remorse. He was feeling bad about the situation he had caused. Then he even says the right words, "*I have sinned.*" So, on the outside everything is looking good and sounding right. But what was going on, on the inside? Was there deep faith? Obviously, the fact that the end choice was suicide reveals Judas had a shallow faith. He was feeling embarrassed. He was sorry he got caught. He was feeling bad about the consequences of his actions, but he was more concerned about himself than he was about God. I do think he felt bad about what he had done to Jesus but not to a large enough degree. The overwhelming feeling was one of self-pity. Poor, poor me! For Judas, suicide was the ultimate way of not taking responsibility, the ultimate way out of a painful time, and the ultimate way out of being overwhelmed by life. When it came down to his faith concerning life, death and God, his real convictions were not developed in a deep enough way to carry him through this defining time in his life.

Peter's story ends differently. He also blew it terribly. He even promised Jesus he would never leave him and that he would be the one who would die for him. He ended up running away and going back to his old life of fishing. After Jesus' death, burial and resurrection, he came looking for Peter. This was going to be a challenging time for Peter. He knew he was in trouble. He knew he had really messed up and would be confronted. Jesus came along the water's edge and made breakfast. Peter recognized him and jumped into the water. If you think about it, he could have jumped on either side of the boat—coming to Jesus or trying to get away from Jesus!

Let's face it. None of us like having to deal with our sins. We don't enjoy being confronted. We don't look forward to seeing our real selves. In our sinful nature we want to run away (or swim away!). But Peter had enough depth to his convictions and faith to fight all those feelings. He wanted to be close to Jesus more than he wanted to protect himself.

> *When they had finished eating, Jesus said to Simon Peter, "Simon son of John, do you truly love me more than these?"*
>
> *"Yes, Lord," he said, "you know that I love you."*
>
> *Jesus said, "Feed my lambs."*
>
> *Again Jesus said, "Simon son of John, do you truly love me?"*
>
> *He answered, "Yes, Lord, you know that I love you."*
>
> *Jesus said, "Take care of my sheep."*
>
> *The third time he said to him, "Simon son of John, do you love me?"*
>
> *Peter was hurt because Jesus asked him the third time, "Do you love me?" He said, "Lord, you know all things; you know that I love you."*
>
> *Jesus said, "Feed my sheep. I tell you the truth, when you were younger you dressed yourself and went where you wanted; but when you are old you will stretch out your hands, and someone else will dress you and lead you where you do not want to go." Jesus said this to indicate the kind of death by which Peter would glorify God. Then he said to him, "Follow me!" (John 21:15–19)*

This was a painful conversation. Jesus said, "*Do you truly love* (agape) *me more than these?*" Peter replied, "*You know that I love* (phileo) *you.*" Jesus was not asking if Peter loved him more than the other apostles, he was asking if he loved him more than his old life—the boats, the nets, the fish, the comfort level, the familiarity, the lack of responsibility. *Agape* is one of the Greek words for love. With this word Jesus was asking, "Do you love me unconditionally? Are you sold out completely? Are you totally committed? Are you willing to die for me?" Peter answered with another Greek word for love; he used the word *phileo*. This is a friendship or family kind of love. Peter basically said, "I'll be your friend."

Again Jesus asked, *"Do you truly love* (agape) *me?"* and again Peter replied, *"You know that I love* (phileo) *you."* Then Jesus changed gears and asked, *"Do you love* (phileo) *me?"* In other words, Jesus said, "Are you even my friend?" or "Do you really care about me?" This hurt Peter. Obviously, Jesus was making a strong point for a good reason. You denied me *three times* so I need to ask you three times! And even more than that, Jesus was making the point that to be his friend and to be in a right relationship with him, the price is an unconditional, sold out, totally committed, faithful-till-death kind of friendship. Then Jesus went on to tell Peter that he would die for the cause if he chose to follow him. WOW! This is certainly a conversation Peter never forgot.

Beyond the basic questions being asked, what was Jesus calling Peter to? Three times Jesus said it: *"feed my lambs...take care of my sheep...feed my sheep."* Feeding and caring for God's sheep is leadership. This was Peter's call back into both a right relationship and into leadership. Jesus was saying it's time again to be the sacrificial leader you were always meant to be. For emphasis, he said to Peter again that it was time to be the sacrificial leader he had the potential to be. And for even greater emphasis, he said for the third time that it was time to decide to be the sacrificial leader he was called to be! And Peter became a game-changing leader as an apostle, elder and evangelist.

What a difference between how Judas handled himself and how Peter handled himself. Night and day! What's the real difference? It's the depth of convictions. It's the depth of faith that had been developed through the years. Peter, like Judas, also felt remorse. He had his time of tears. He said many of the right words. But instead of primarily hurting for himself, he was primarily hurting for Jesus. And so, he was willing to take correction and then change direction.

There's one more thing to take note of in this passage of Scripture before we leave it:

> *Peter turned and saw that the disciple whom Jesus loved was following them. (This was the one who had leaned back against Jesus at the supper and had said, "Lord, who is going to betray you?") When Peter saw him, he asked, "Lord, what about him?" (John 20–21)*

Just like us, Peter still had a ways to go. He turned to Jesus and said, "If I have to die then what about John? Let's be fair here. If I die then he dies too!" So what's the point? The point is that Peter still had to work things out in his head and work things through in his heart even as he was going to be this incredible leader in God's kingdom. We must not compare our sacrifices, our situations, our pains and our loads with those of other Christians. Let God decide what each person must sacrifice and face in this life. All we can do is to keep ourselves in the fight and keep ourselves building deep convictions—building a deep faith.

## CLEAR CONVICTIONS

author unknown /adapted

I'm part of the fellowship of the unashamed. I have Holy Spirit power. The die is cast. I have stepped over the line. The decision has been made. I'm a disciple of His. I won't look back, let up, slow down, back away or be still.

My past is redeemed, my present makes sense, my future is secure. I'm finished with low living, sight walking, small planning, smooth knees, colorless dreams, tamed visions, mundane thinking, "chintzy" giving and dwarfed goals.

I no longer need preeminence, prosperity, position, promotions, plaudits or popularity. I don't have to be right, first, tops, recognized, praised, regarded or rewarded. I now live by presence, lean by faith, walk by patience, lift by prayer and labor by power.

My face is set, my gait is fast, my goal is heaven, my road is narrow, my way is rough, my companions few, my Guide reliable, my mission clear. I cannot be bought, compromised, detoured, lured away, turned back, deluded or delayed. I will not flinch in the face of sacrifice, hesitate in the presence of the adversary, negotiate at the table of the enemy, ponder at the pool of popularity or meander in the maze of mediocrity.

I won't give up, shut up, let up until I have stayed up, stored up, prayed up, paid up, preached up for the cause of Christ. I am a disciple of Jesus. I must go until He comes, give until I drop, preach until all know and work until He stops me.

And when He comes for His own, He will have no problem recognizing me—**MY CONVICTIONS WILL BE CLEAR!**

## Conclusion: What Is a Deep Conviction?

A deep conviction for disciples is a Bible truth, a Bible belief that we hold so dear that no one and no thing can move us from it. It affects every area of our lives—how we think, how we act, how we react, how we feel. As we have previously stated, it's just another way of talking about faith. The depth of a person's convictions is the depth of a person's faith. Let's go on to learn how to build a deep faith with the 10 FAITH SECRETS.

PART THREE

# SECRETS OF FAITH

# FAITH SECRET 1

## God's Word and Potential Faith

*Consequently, faith comes from hearing the message, and the message is heard through* ***the word*** *about Christ. (Romans 10:17, emphasis added)*

*For* ***the word of God*** *is alive and active. Sharper than any double-edged sword, it penetrates even to dividing soul and spirit, joints and marrow; it judges the thoughts and attitudes of the heart. Nothing in all creation is hidden from God's sight. Everything is uncovered and laid bare before the eyes of him to whom we must give account. (Hebrews 4:12–13, emphasis added)*

*Sanctify them by the truth;* ***your word*** *is truth. (John 17:17, emphasis added)*

*And we also thank God continually because, when you received* ***the word of God,*** *which you heard from us, you accepted it not as a human word, but as it actually is,* ***the word of God,*** *which is indeed at work in you who believe. (1 Thessalonians 2:13, emphasis added)*

The first faith secret is this: know where to go to get faith! In accordance with Romans 10:17 we must go to the word of God for our source of faith. The amount of God's word (Bible) stored in our heart and mind is a measure of our potential faith. This is a *potential* amount and not an actual amount. It is not actual faith until we "act" on what we know.

Saving faith has three components. First, there must be the intellectual agreement to the facts. Second, there must be a trust in the promises. And third, there must be obedience to the commands. There must be a combination of all of these components or it is not a biblical faith—it is not a saving faith. But where do we learn the facts? They are in the word of God—the Bible. Where do we learn about all the wonderful promises that we are to put our trust in? They are in the word of God—the Bible. Where do we learn what the commands of God are and how to obey them? Again, this is found in the word of God—the Bible.

I can gain faith that there is a God just by looking at his creation. As I look at the order and the complexity of this universe, it only makes sense to believe that there is a mind, an intelligence, behind the design. After all, who would look at a painting of a beautiful landscape and say it just happened...it just appeared on the wall? No one in their right mind would believe such a thing! Because there is order to the painting, there would have to be a mind behind it. And so it is with the much more intricate creation of our bodies, our planet and our universe. I can also gain faith that there is a God by seeing the effect of God's power in the lives of the people around me. As I am around those who are radically changed and who are lovingly unified through their relationship with God, I can know that he exists and that he can also change me. But neither the creation itself nor seeing the effects of God's power in people's lives can communicate to me who God is or what the nature of God is or what his will is for my life. This is where the word of God comes into play. From the Bible and only from the Bible can I know who this creator God is, and only from the Bible can I learn how to live the way I was created to live.

Jesus is the living Word—God's ultimate communication in the flesh to us about love and life. Now he continues to communicate this to us through the written "living" word that we know as the Bible. The claim of the Bible is that the Spirit of God searched the mind of God and then revealed it to certain men at certain times. God had these men write down his revelation so that all could have truth and understand certain mysteries about God and man. And most definitely, if God can create and sustain his universe, he can create and sustain his book for all men for all time!

*For since the creation of the world God's invisible qualities — his eternal power and divine nature — have been clearly seen, being understood from what has been made, so that people are without excuse. (Romans 1:20)*

*Above all, you must understand that no prophecy of Scripture came about by the prophet's own interpretation of things. For prophecy never had its origin in the human will, but prophets, though human, spoke from God as they were carried along by the Holy Spirit. (2 Peter 1:20–21)*

Unfortunately, "faith" for most people in our world today does not exclusively come from the word of God. Most people in the world base their faith (knowledge of God and of his will) either on their feelings, on their family tradition, on a personal experience or on what a religious leader tells them to believe. Let's think about all of this.

First of all, feelings are always up and down. They are never constant. This makes feelings a terrible standard for truth. Feeling close or connected to God does not make us that way. Even feeling distant and disconnected from God does not necessarily mean it's true. I may have a great feeling about a test I take, but my feelings are not the standard for the grade I will receive. I could feel bad and the grade turn out good. Or I could feel good and the grade turn out bad. I may have feelings, even strong feelings, about a particular person and yet they may not even know who I am. That scenario actually happened to me back in my college days when I asked a girl out on a date after a church service. She answered, "And what was your name again?" That was embarrassing! I had been thinking about her and had developed some feelings for her even without really knowing her. I miscalculated (to say the least) her feelings about me—she did not even know my name! Feelings certainly do not make a relationship real.

Let's now move on to family traditions. The tradition may even be many generations old, but the longevity of something untrue does not eventually create something true. A family tradition is neither right nor wrong just because it is a family tradition. It must be weighed by the word of God, since that is the standard for truth. Jesus was quite upset with those in his time who considered their traditions of greater importance than the word of God.

> *He replied, "Isaiah was right when he prophesied about you hypocrites; as it is written:*
>
> *'These people honor me with their lips,*
> *but their hearts are far from me.*
> *They worship me in vain;*
> *their teachings are merely human rules.'*
>
> *You have let go of the commands of God and are holding on to human traditions. . . .*
> *"Thus you nullify the word of God by your tradition that you have handed down. And you do many things like that." (Mark 7:6–8, 13)*

There are also those who base their faith on experiences. One example of this was back on the campus of the University of South Carolina when I served as a campus minister. I was studying the Bible with a student who based his faith in God on an experience he believed he had. He said he was out on a dock late one night praying to God about his salvation. He then looked up into the sky and the clouds formed the word "YES." Now personally, I have "seen" many things in the clouds. I just need to use a little imagination. The other problem is that I don't find anywhere in the Bible telling me to expect this experience. Experiences are not valid unless they are validated by the word of God. I can't base my faith on an experience that I believe I have had. Otherwise any experience that anyone has is valid and true simply because they choose to believe it. The interesting thing about the student I was studying with was how he was living. He was a party guy—premarital sex and drunkenness was his way of life. The word of God does have a few things to say about this kind of behavior.

> *The acts of the flesh are obvious: sexual immorality, impurity and debauchery; idolatry and witchcraft; hatred, discord, jealousy, fits of rage, selfish ambition, dissensions, factions and envy; drunkenness, orgies, and the like. I warn you, as I did before, that those who live like this will not inherit the kingdom of God. (Galatians 5:19–21).*

And so there is a clear and absolute moral standard found in the word of God, and yet, because of this student's experience, he believed he was forever saved. For him, as with so many, his experience trumped the word of God. As I have been in the full-time ministry for over thirty-five years, I have been told about many of these "experiences." Some of the experiences have to do with being healed by God or having certain prayers being answered by him. This becomes the basis of a person's faith. Certainly God heals and certainly God answers prayer (even for those not in a right relationship with him). These kinds of experiences should send us to search for God and to find true faith from his word, not necessarily to think that all is well with us spiritually. Each person must go to the Bible and find out the truth about themselves and about God's plan for their lives.

Finally, let us consider the use of a religious leader as our source of faith. A religious leader may be sincere, but sincerity does not create truth. Just because I sincerely believe that gravity does not exist does not make it that way. If I jump off a ten-story building I will still be scraped off the sidewalk, regardless of the intensity of my sincerity that there is no such thing as gravity. The law of gravity exists whether I believe it or not! And so it is with God's laws: they exist whether I believe them or not. Certainly Paul was a sincere religious leader. Before being taught and having faith in Christ, he was a religious leader who was sincerely wrong, as he put Christians in jail and had some killed. It is interesting to note that while Paul was preaching in Berea, those listening to him did not simply believe him about Jesus and salvation. They went back to the Old Testament Scriptures (the completed New Testament was not in existence yet) to make sure of the truth. The result of getting into God's word was faith!

> *Now the Berean Jews were of more noble character than those in Thessalonica, for they received the message with great eagerness and examined the Scriptures every day to see if what Paul said was true. As a result, many of them believed, as did also a number of prominent Greek women and many Greek men. (Acts 17:11–12)*

Therefore, faith cannot be based on or come from feelings, traditions, experiences or the teachings of religious leaders. Furthermore, we find that our faith potential is proportionate to the amount of God's word that is stored in our heart and mind. This is Faith Secret 1! The exciting aspect of this secret is that we determine for ourselves the degree of our potential faith:

**Little Word of God = Little Potential Faith**
**No Word of God = No Potential Faith**
**Much Word of God = Much Potential Faith**

God deeply desires to place the gift of faith in our hearts, and it is through the reading, hearing, studying, meditation and memorization of Scripture that we determine our potential faith.

## Three Parables of the Sower

Let's look at the Parable of the Sower. There is much to learn about the word of God from this earthly story with a heavenly meaning. Just like us with our favorite stories, Jesus told this parable many times. And just as we never tell a story exactly the same way twice, neither did Jesus. We actually find this parable recorded for us three different times, although I am sure he did his "Sower Study" many more times than that!

> *While a large crowd was gathering and people were coming to Jesus from town after town, he told this parable: "A farmer went out to sow his seed. As he was scattering*

> *the seed, some fell along the path; it was trampled on, and the birds ate it up. Some fell on rocky ground, and when it came up, the plants withered because they had no moisture. Other seed fell among thorns, which grew up with it and choked the plants. Still other seed fell on good soil. It came up and yielded a crop, a hundred times more than was sown." (Luke 8:4–8)*

Then Jesus tells us the meaning of the parable.

> *"This is the meaning of the parable: The seed is the word of God. Those along the path are the ones who hear, and then the devil comes and takes away the word from their hearts, so that they may not believe and be saved. Those on the rocky ground are the ones who receive the word with joy when they hear it, but they have no root. They believe for a while, but in the time of testing they fall away. The seed that fell among thorns stands for those who hear, but as they go on their way they are choked by life's worries, riches and pleasures, and they do not mature. But the seed on good soil stands for those with a noble and good heart, who hear the word, retain it, and by persevering produce a crop." (Luke 8:11–15)*

In this parable, we find the farmer sowing his seed in different types of soils. To be more accurate, this really should be named the Parable of the Hearts. Each "*soil*" describes a type of heart that exists in all people everywhere. There is the hard heart, the shallow heart, the entangled heart and the good heart. For our immediate discussion, the most important ingredient in this story is the stated fact that the "*seed*" is the "*word of God.*" Now, remember as we discuss this parable of Jesus that the word of God releases our potential faith.

When the seed (word of God) is placed on the path which represents the hard heart, it does not penetrate and so there is no faith. A person's heart can be so hardened by their pride and sin that it will not even listen to the word of God. When the seed (the word of God) is placed on the rocky ground, which represents the shallow heart, this heart believes only for a short time because the root system does not go deep. It is interesting to note that the word of God did produce faith. It was the person's heart decision to not take the word in deeply that ultimately destroyed the faith. These people quickly fall away in the time of testing, especially due to persecutions.

When the seed (the word of God) is in the thorns, which represent the entangled heart, it does not mature. In the telling of this parable by Matthew, it states that certain thorns would choke the word. So again we find that the seed or word of God produces faith, but this type of person allows the word of God to be choked out. The faith potential is lost because of the bad choice in priorities and desires that do not allow time with the word of God. The specific list of *"thorns"* from Matthew 13, Mark 4 and Luke 8 includes: *"the worries of this life," "the deceitfulness of wealth," "the desires for other things"* and *"life's worries, riches and pleasures."* And so we see, the less into God's word a person is, the less that person's potential faith.

The final type of soil is the good soil, which represents the good heart. This person retains the word of God and perseveres in it. Doing this ensures a consistent protection and a consistent building of faith. And with this kind of consistent, growing faith, a person's life will make a definitive difference and will impact the world! And so the seed is the word of God, and the word of God is the source of our potential faith.

This analogy is amazing! It illustrates the power of the word of God to produce faith. Imagine an acorn...one seed. Inside that tiny acorn is the power to produce a giant oak tree that can live for hundreds of years. God does not come down and miraculously zap each individual acorn with the power of life. He has already placed the potential power in every acorn to produce a tree. So it is with faith. God does not come and miraculously zap an individual with faith. He has already placed the power of life (faith) into his seed—his word—the Bible. If we allow the seed (God's word) to be planted in our hearts, it will produce faith. And if we allow God's word to grow deep and to grow consistently in our hearts, our faith will be strong, vibrant and fruitful. The word of God gives the potential to produce a strong, godly man or woman who is in a right relationship with God through faith and who will live with him forever!

## Manna

*He humbled you, causing you to hunger and then feeding you with manna, which neither you nor your ancestors had known, to teach you that man does not live on bread alone but on every word that comes from the mouth of the LORD. (Deuteronomy 8:3)*

So often, the realities in the seen world reveal the realities in the unseen world. God taught the Israelites to gain faith through the daily provision and daily gathering of manna—bread from heaven. (Note: God provided it for them daily except on the Sabbath when it would last two days due to the no-work ordinance). They could not live (physically) without the manna. His ultimate goal was to teach the Israelites to daily gain faith through the word of God. They were to learn that they could not live (spiritually) without it. And yes, just like manna, the word of God is miraculously provided by God for us. Could I live physically without food for a day? For a week? For a month? The answer is yes, but I would grow weaker and weaker as time went on. I have in fact done two thirty-day fasts in my life. I drank water and juices only. I certainly did grow weaker physically. I did not have the same kind of stamina. Eventually, if a person does not eat, he will die. This is also true spiritually. Can I live without the word of God for a day? For a week? For a month? Yes, but faith grows weaker and weaker and eventually will die. I am made by God to eat food every day. In fact, I eat more than once a day. I am also made by God to be nourished by the word of God every day. It's the only way for faith to stay healthy, strong and alive. Faith comes from the word of God...this is my faith potential!

When I was studying to become a Christian, it was so awesome to just look at the Bible and only the Bible as the basis of my faith. In my first year as a Christian, I took two classes offered at church that deepened and rooted my faith, one on the book of Acts and then one on the book of Romans. As a part of these classes, I memorized about eighty scriptures. This is why my faith grew so much during that time. I started to actually have God's word living inside me, in my heart and in my mind. Since our potential faith is from God's word, my potential faith went sky high.

As I have already stated, I have been a Christian for forty-two years at the time of writing this book. There have been certain years in my life when I had a definitive plan to read through the Bible. Other years I have studied certain books or certain topics. Presently, I am taking the year and studying the book of Proverbs. If it's the first of the month, I read chapter 1. If it's the fifteenth of the month, then I am on chapter 15. I choose a particular passage that grabs my heart and I meditate on it, striving to keep it in my heart for the whole day. By the end of the year I will have gone through all of the Proverbs twelve times! That's a lot of great faith potential about practical, godly living. And on top of it being the right thing to do, it's both a mental and an emotional stimulation...and it's a lot of fun. A while ago, Kay and I went to a Caribbean island to celebrate our wedding anniversary. Each morning after breakfast we sat together looking at the clear, aquamarine-colored ocean, reading and talking about a chapter from the book of Proverbs. It's nice to grow closer together as you grow together in faith!

And so we have Faith Secret 1. Our potential faith is directly proportional to the amount of the word of God we place upon our hearts. Therefore...

**Little Word of God = Little Potential Faith**
**No Word of God = No Potential Faith**
**Much Word of God = Much Potential Faith**

# FAITH SECRET 2

## Humility and Potential Faith

*When Jesus had entered Capernaum, a centurion came to him, asking for help. "Lord," he said, "my servant lies at home paralyzed, suffering terribly."*

*Jesus said to him, "Shall I come and heal him?"*

*The centurion replied, "Lord, I do not deserve to have you come under my roof. But just say the word, and my servant will be healed. For I myself am a man under authority, with soldiers under me. I tell this one, 'Go,' and he goes; and that one, 'Come,' and he comes. I say to my servant, 'Do this,' and he does it."*

*When Jesus heard this, he was amazed and said to those following him, "Truly I tell you, I have not found anyone in Israel with such great faith." (Matthew 8:5–10)*

The centurion had the key to the second faith secret: humility. His heart was revealed when he stated that he did not deserve Jesus taking the time to come to his home. He saw himself as *totally* undeserving. Also, the centurion understood Jesus as one who is under authority and who also commands authority. More than that, he was willing to be completely submissive to Jesus' authority. Jesus was astonished by this man's radical faith. It was greater faith than what he had found in all of Israel. He was positively excited and probably thinking, "At last, one who really believes in me and who truly trusts in me!" I can imagine a big smile on Jesus' face as he walked away from this situation. We must be like this man, knowing we deserve absolutely nothing while knowing God can do absolutely everything.

And so, another faith potential and our second faith secret is found in the degree of our heart's humility before God. To that degree we can be filled with faith. Faith is humbling ourselves under

God's authority and love. This allows us contact with God and his unlimited power. Our potential faith is a product of our humility. As pride and self-sufficiency go out, faith can come in! Therefore, the second faith secret can be shown as:

**Little Humility = Little Potential Faith**
**No Humility = No Potential Faith**
**Much Humility = Much Potential Faith**

Before anyone can start to be filled up with faith, they must embrace a deep sense of inadequacy. They must know they are helpless to save themselves or to change themselves. As this is accomplished, humility or meekness (not weakness!) can invade the heart and open the door for faith to enter and live. Radical faith is the willingness to submit, follow and obey the word of God. Until I know I am in need of God, I keep the door to radical faith closed. God is always at work in everyone's life to help them understand the need for his power, wisdom and guidance. Our pride must be broken down and broken through. The greater our pride, the harder God has to strike to get our attention. Either we break or we get broken. Nebuchadnezzar and Belshazzar are the Bible poster kids for this!

## Nebuchadnezzar

*I, Nebuchadnezzar, was at home in my palace, contented and prosperous. I had a dream that made me afraid. As I was lying in bed, the images and visions that passed through my mind terrified me. So I commanded that all the wise men of Babylon be brought before me to interpret the dream for me. When the magicians, enchanters, astrologers and diviners came, I told them the dream, but they could not interpret it for me. Finally, Daniel came into my presence and I told him the dream. (He is called Belteshazzar, after the name of my god, and the spirit of the holy gods is in him.) (Daniel 4:4–8)*

Nebuchadnezzar became king of Babylon, the most powerful

nation of the time, in 605 BC. Therefore, Nebuchadnezzar was the most powerful man on the face of the earth. He was not just a king; he was the king of all kings! God worked in a remarkable way in his life to humble him and open his faith potential. He was rich, powerful, contented and comfortable. Nevertheless, he had a dream that terrified him. God has a way of comforting the disturbed and disturbing the comfortable! To explain his dream, Nebuchadnezzar sent for Daniel, a young Jewish man who was in captivity, having been forcibly taken from his homeland. Daniel was a prophet of God.

> *Then Daniel (also called Belteshazzar) was greatly perplexed for a time, and his thoughts terrified him. So the king said, "Belteshazzar, do not let the dream or its meaning alarm you."*
>
> *Belteshazzar answered, "My lord, if only the dream applied to your enemies and its meaning to your adversaries! The tree you saw, which grew large and strong, with its top touching the sky, visible to the whole earth, with beautiful leaves and abundant fruit, providing food for all, giving shelter to the wild animals, and having nesting places in its branches for the birds — Your Majesty, you are that tree! You have become great and strong; your greatness has grown until it reaches the sky, and your dominion extends to distant parts of the earth.*
>
> *"Your Majesty saw a holy one, a messenger, coming down from heaven and saying, 'Cut down the tree and destroy it, but leave the stump, bound with iron and bronze, in the grass of the field, while its roots remain in the ground. Let him be drenched with the dew of heaven; let him live with the wild animals, until seven times pass by for him.'" (Daniel 4:19–23)*

Ultimately, Nebuchadnezzar is to learn who he is and who God is... "*that the living may know that the Most High is sovereign over all kingdoms on earth and gives them to anyone he wishes and sets over them the lowliest of people*" (4:17). Then Nebuchadnezzar was to tell everyone what he had learned! Certainly the king of kings would have a voice that people would listen to. But, as it ends up, he does not just speak to his own generation; his words are recorded for us in the Bible. This becomes a proclamation to all mankind for all time. God used a man outside the borders of his kingdom to speak to the world in every generation!

> *"This is the interpretation, Your Majesty, and this is the decree the Most High has issued against my lord the king: You will be driven away from people and will live with the wild animals; you will eat grass like the ox and be drenched with the dew of heaven. Seven times will pass by for you until you acknowledge that the Most High is sovereign over all kingdoms on earth and gives them to anyone he wishes. The command to leave the stump of the tree with its roots means that your kingdom will be restored to you when you acknowledge that Heaven rules. Therefore, Your Majesty, be pleased to accept my advice: Renounce your sins by doing what is right, and your wickedness by being kind to the oppressed. It may be that then your prosperity will continue." (Daniel 4:24–27)*

Seven represents the number for God in Jewish thought—the perfect number. So what is being said here? He would live with wild animals for the *perfect* amount of time (some think seven actual years) until he gets it...who he is and who God is. Then he was to proclaim to the whole world what he had learned. Again and again it is stated that seven times (the perfect amount of time needed) would pass until Nebuchadnezzar would acknowledge that heaven rules—*and not Nebuchadnezzar!* He would live like a wild animal. He would be out of his mind, because anyone who thinks they are the center of the universe is out of their minds! When we are not thinking right about who we are and who God is, we are living the life of an animal instead of living the life of a beloved creature made in the image of God. This is what God is always striving to tell and to teach every one of us. God is always at work trying to bring us back to him—to get us back in our right minds! And in this passage Daniel is telling one of the most powerful and most ruthless kings in history to take his advice. The king needed to repent. He needed to change his life. He needed to start doing what was right, to start caring a lot more about the poor and needy and a lot less about himself. It took great courage for Daniel to tell this to the king. And apparently, it made some degree of difference for about twelve months. But then Nebuchadnezzar's true heart came out, for what comes out of a man's mouth is from his heart.

> *All this happened to King Nebuchadnezzar. Twelve months later, as the king was walking on the roof of the royal palace of Babylon, he said, "Is not this the great Babylon I have built as the royal residence, by my mighty power and for the glory of my majesty?"*
>
> *Even as the words were on his lips, a voice came from heaven, "This is what is decreed for you, King Nebuchadnezzar: Your royal authority has been taken from you. You will be driven away from people and will live with the wild animals; you will eat grass like the ox. Seven times will pass by for you until you acknowledge that the Most High is sovereign over all kingdoms on earth and gives them to anyone he wishes."*
>
> *Immediately what had been said about Nebuchadnezzar was fulfilled. He was driven away from people and ate grass like the ox. His body was drenched with the dew of heaven until his hair grew like the feathers of an eagle and his nails like the claws of a bird. (Daniel 4:28–33)*

Recorded here are some of the scariest words in the Bible: "*even as the words were on his lips.*" God hears us and knows the arrogance, self-sufficiency and self-congratulation embedded deep within our hearts. Then God hits hard and fast—not to hurt, but to help. Until Nebuchadnezzar acknowledged that **God is Sovereign** over all kingdoms on earth and gives them to anyone he wishes, he would be away from his sanity, his honor and his splendor. And so it is with us. Until we acknowledge that God is in control and that everything we have going for us is from God, we live an insane life away from the honor and splendor of living as we were created to live. Only when Nebuchadnezzar embraced a deep sense of inadequacy and had a willingness to come under God's authority could he have potential faith. He could now look up and see clearly. His eyes were off himself. His eyes could "see" God.

> *At the end of that time, I, Nebuchadnezzar, raised my eyes toward heaven, and my sanity was restored. Then I praised the Most High; I honored and glorified him who lives forever.*
>
> *His dominion is an eternal dominion;*

*his kingdom endures from generation to generation.*
*All the peoples of the earth*
*are regarded as nothing.*
*He does as he pleases*
*with the powers of heaven*
*and the peoples of the earth.*
*No one can hold back his hand*
*or say to him: "What have you done?"*

*At the same time that my sanity was restored, my honor and splendor were returned to me for the glory of my kingdom. My advisers and nobles sought me out, and I was restored to my throne and became even greater than before. Now I, Nebuchadnezzar, praise and exalt and glorify the King of heaven, because everything he does is right and all his ways are just. And those who walk in pride he is able to humble. (Daniel 4:34–37)*

Now Nebuchadnezzar knows! Now he gets it! God has done it—brought him from being a prideful man to being a humble man. He understands that God is everything and that he is nothing. And so, Nebuchadnezzar became open to having faith in God—his new-found humility gave him a great potential faith. He went on and actualized his faith by his obedience in proclaiming to the world that God is the one true God. He proclaimed for all time that God is supreme, is in control, is always right and is always just. And so it is true: much humility = much faith potential.

## Belshazzar

*King Belshazzar gave a great banquet for a thousand of his nobles and drank wine with them. While Belshazzar was drinking his wine, he gave orders to bring in the gold and silver goblets that Nebuchadnezzar his father had taken from the temple in Jerusalem, so that the king and his nobles, his wives and his concubines might drink from them. So they brought in the gold goblets that had been taken from the temple of God in Jerusalem, and the king and his nobles, his wives and his concubines drank from them. As they drank the wine, they praised the gods of gold and silver, of bronze, iron, wood and stone.*

*Suddenly the fingers of a human hand appeared and wrote on the plaster of the wall, near the lampstand in the royal palace. The king watched the hand as it wrote. His face turned pale and he was so frightened that his legs became weak and his knees were knocking.*

> *The king summoned the enchanters, astrologers and diviners. Then he said to these wise men of Babylon, "Whoever reads this writing and tells me what it means will be clothed in purple and have a gold chain placed around his neck, and he will be made the third highest ruler in the kingdom." (Daniel 5:1–7)*

We have all heard the phrase, "the handwriting's on the wall." Well, this is where the whole world gets that saying! Belshazzar was related to Nebuchadnezzar, his distant father, probably his grandfather. Belshazzar's father, Nabonidus, probably married a daughter of Nebuchadnezzar. Belshazzar himself was a crown prince and was in place to rule as a king even while his father was still the king. That is why he could only offer Daniel the honor of being *third* in rank in the Babylonian kingdom if he interpreted the handwriting on the wall. The year is now 539 BC. While Belshazzar is throwing a party to impress his guests, he brings out objects from the treasury that were taken from the temple in Jerusalem forty-seven years earlier. He is full of himself and full of false gods. He certainly knew all that his grandfather had proclaimed about the one true God, but he did not listen and he did not care. He was full of pride, but God got his attention.

> *Then all the king's wise men came in, but they could not read the writing or tell the king what it meant. So King Belshazzar became even more terrified and his face grew more pale. His nobles were baffled.*
>
> *The queen, hearing the voices of the king and his nobles, came into the banquet hall. "May the king live forever!" she said. "Don't be alarmed! Don't look so pale! There is a man in your kingdom who has the spirit of the holy gods in him. In the time of your father he was found to have insight and intelligence and wisdom like that of the gods. Your father, King Nebuchadnezzar, appointed him chief of the magicians, enchanters, astrologers and diviners. He did this because Daniel, whom the king called Belteshazzar, was found to have a keen mind and knowledge and understanding, and also the ability to interpret dreams, explain riddles and solve difficult problems. Call for Daniel, and he will tell you what the writing means." (Daniel 5:8–12)*

And so Daniel comes before Belshazzar. I am sure that Daniel came with a smile in his heart saying to himself, "So, here we go again!" He had been here before with his old friend "Neb" or Nebuchadnezzar. (I think he must have gotten on pretty friendly terms with him through the years!) He was now standing in front of the grandson who had such a different heart.

> *Then Daniel answered the king, "You may keep your gifts for yourself and give your rewards to someone else. Nevertheless, I will read the writing for the king and tell him what it means.*
>
> *"Your Majesty, the Most High God gave your father Nebuchadnezzar sovereignty and greatness and glory and splendor. Because of the high position he gave him, all the nations and peoples of every language dreaded and feared him. Those the king wanted to put to death, he put to death; those he wanted to spare, he spared; those he wanted to promote, he promoted; and those he wanted to humble, he humbled. But when his heart became arrogant and hardened with pride, he was deposed from his royal throne and stripped of his glory. He was driven away from people and given the mind of an animal; he lived with the wild donkeys and ate grass like the ox; and his body was drenched with the dew of heaven, until he acknowledged that the Most High God is sovereign over all kingdoms on earth and sets over them anyone he wishes.*
>
> *"But you, Belshazzar, his son, have not humbled yourself, though you knew all this. Instead, you have set yourself up against the Lord of heaven. You had the goblets from his temple brought to you, and you and your nobles, your wives and your concubines drank wine from them. You praised the gods of silver and gold, of bronze, iron, wood and stone, which cannot see or hear or understand. But you did not honor the God who holds in his hand your life and all your ways. Therefore he sent the hand that wrote the inscription." (Daniel 5:17–24)*

WOW, Daniel! That's not a good way to keep your head on your shoulders! Consider Daniel's words to the King: *You* have not humbled yourself! *You* were given opportunities and *you* knew the truth. *You* set yourself up against God. *You* did what you knew was wrong. *You* did not honor God with your life. There was no way Belshazzar missed what Daniel was saying to him.

> *"This is the inscription that was written:*
>
> *MENE, MENE, TEKEL, PARSIN*
>
> *"Here is what these words mean:*
>
> Mene: *God has numbered the days of your reign and brought it to an end.*

> Tekel: *You have been weighed on the scales and found wanting.*
> Parsin: *Your kingdom is divided and given to the Medes and Persians."*
>
> *Then at Belshazzar's command, Daniel was clothed in purple, a gold chain was placed around his neck, and he was proclaimed the third highest ruler in the kingdom.*
>
> *That very night Belshazzar, king of the Babylonians, was slain, and Darius the Mede took over the kingdom, at the age of sixty-two. (Daniel 5:25–31)*

This is sobering. There comes a time when we must pay the consequences for the life choices we make. Although God sets up and allows many situations to come into our lives to humble us, our response remains our choice. The Bible says Belshazzar never humbled *himself*. He never took a deep look inside himself to "see" who he really was and he never looked up to "see" who God really is. What happened to Nebuchadnezzar was epic. What happened to Belshazzar was tragic. The end result is always predicated on each individual's choice. With Belshazzar we dramatically see the truth of the second faith secret: no humility = no potential faith.

## The Handwriting on My Wall

Nebuchadnezzar had a dream and was terrified. Belshazzar had the writing on the wall and was terrified. There was also a time in my life when I was terrified. It was when the doctor told me I had Hodgkin's disease or cancer of the lymph nodes. The big C! I had just turned seventeen a few weeks prior to this, in February 1973. I was a senior in high school and thought I had the world by the tail. Most everything in my life was going in the right direction. I was no sports or scholastic superstar, but I was happy. I had good friends. I dated some of the pretty and popular girls. I felt good about myself—my looks and my intellect. I was planning to go to college. I had my hopes and my dreams. I wanted to become a lawyer and be a writer. I even had some faith in God and thought all was good in that department of life.

And then I found myself in an operating room having thoracic surgery. My chest was cracked open so the tumor between my heart and my lung (about the size of my fist) could be removed. Weeks later I had to go under the knife again for exploratory surgery. Cutting from the bottom of my sternum past my belly button, the surgeon took a biopsy of different tissues and organs to see if the cancer was contained or if it had spread. (And what a great look when the two operation scars go from top to bottom on your chest and stomach!) On top of this, there was a battery of painful procedures and tests to undergo. And finally there were rounds of cobalt radiation treatment. At my worst, I fell to the weight of only 117 pounds. I was weak and sleeping many hours a day. I didn't look good and I didn't feel good. In the end, the cancer was contained. It was caught early in stage one. All in all, it was about five months from the first operation to the last cobalt treatment. Even with all of this, the doctors said they would not pronounce me cured until five years had passed with no reoccurrence of the cancer. It has now been over forty-two years. But at the time, I was terrified. And since I had plenty of pride, I look back and figure that God had to hit me pretty hard to humble me. Without all of this, I would not have been so open to the word of God. I would not have been so ready to obey what I learned from the Bible. In the end, I made the choice to humble *myself* and submit to God.

> *Or do you think Scripture says without reason that he jealously longs for the spirit he has caused to dwell in us? But he gives us more grace. That is why Scripture says:*
>
> *"God opposes the proud*
> *but shows favor to the humble."*
>
> *Submit yourselves, then, to God. . . Humble yourselves before the Lord, and he will lift you up. (James 4:5–7a, 10)*

God is always at work in our lives. He wants us to have a radical faith that impacts this world and will take us home to be with him forever. He works through different people and different situations at different times of our lives trying to humble us so we can be open to his word and to potential faith. It may not be as extreme as Nebuchadnezzar's insanity. It might not be as bizarre as Belshazzar's finger-painting party. It might not be as severe as my cancer. But we should be listening, because God is trying to get our attention. Due to our pride and self-sufficiency, we only have certain windows of time in our lives when we are open and humble to the word of God. Most of the time we stay closed, and once one of those windows gets opened, we tend to close it again.

God sets the times and places. I know God set my time and my place. Before moving to the Chicago area, we lived near Orlando. My father was an oral surgeon in the Navy. The plan was for us to stay in Orlando another year and then move to Italy. Due to an emergency personnel situation and the career opportunity it gave to my father, we ended up going to Chicago, where he was stationed at the Great Lakes Naval Hospital. So we moved to an unplanned location and we moved a year ahead of schedule. This brought me to where a shadow on an X-ray was detected and to the place where a world-renowned expert was brought in by the Navy as an outside consultant for two cases of Hodgkin's disease. I was one of those two cases. This is where my father had friends and had influence to have eminent doctors and surgeons work on my case. On top of this, my brother had become a Christian a year earlier. After my five-month ordeal, he was able to share his faith with me and take me to church where I could be taught the Bible. I don't believe this was all circumstantial. I believe the hand of God was at work here just as much as the hand of God was at work on Belshazzar's wall!

An open time to God's word may be the result of a tragedy, a loss, a problem, a challenge or even a great blessing that gets us to see our nothingness and his greatness. God is always trying to get us to look up and "see" him. As we age, we lose more and more of our physical strength. God is saying, "Find your strength in me." When we face death and our bodies are slowly shutting down, this is just God's last attempt at humbling us and showing us our ultimate weakness and our desperate need for him. So, let us get humble and stay humble in this life and not wait to be humbled on the Day of Judgment. We either bow our knee to God now or we will do it later.

And so we have Faith Secret 2. Our potential faith is directly proportional to our heart's humility before God...

**Little Humility = Little Potential Faith**
**No Humility = No Potential Faith**
**Much Humility = Much Potential Faith**

# FAITH SECRET 3

## A God Kind of Faith

*For as he thinks within himself, so he is. (NASB)*
*For as he thinks in his heart, so is he. (NKJV)*
*For as he hath thought in his soul, so is he. (YLT)*

Listen carefully to a person's words and you will quickly know if that person has little or great faith. In the passage above, God gives us a tremendous insight into this.

What we think inside is what our outside reality eventually becomes. In order to do big things, we must first think big thoughts. When a person says "I can't," it's a true statement. As a man "thinks within himself, so he is"! Henry Ford once stated that "If you think you can or if you think you can't, you're right both times." He was 100% correct. The mind that God created and gave to us is a very powerful entity with a great creative and imaginative ability. What the mind believes is possible can become reality, whether it be two brothers flying a plane on a North Carolina beach or a man walking on the moon. A person must visualize before something can be actualized. But, as we will see, there is a big difference in having faith *in self* and having *faith in God*. We need to make sure we are using our minds and the gift of faith correctly and effectively.

Everything we have that man has invented has been from the power of faith. It could be called "imagineering." The printing press. The car. The electric light bulb. The television. The airplane. The atom bomb. The Internet. Cell phones. Computers. Touch screens. The cloud. Each had to be visualized before it could be actualized. The truth is that the awesome power of faith is available to everyone. God created this universe by faith and we are created in his image; therefore, we have the ability to create by faith. There are those who are making millions of dollars every year by writing books and speaking in seminars promoting faith concepts for personal improvement programs and for acquiring material wealth. These people may be worldly, but give them credit—these people are smart! They take what is free and market it slickly and smoothly for great gain. But beware! These self-powered concepts of faith are not just in the business and personal self-improvement books; they have also invaded the religious section of the bookstores and the pulpits of our world. We must understand that the worldly concepts of "believe in yourself," "think positive," "think big," "I can do it" and "I feel great" are all worthless when it comes to our relationship with God. They serve only to pollute and erode true faith in God. Their focus is on self and not on God. It is a self-serving and self-seeking type of religion in which Christianity is lowered to a self-improvement plan and becomes just another aspect of our own selfishness.

## Faith in Self Is Powerful

Back in 1939, there was a man named George Dantzig, who was a doctoral candidate at the University of California, Berkeley. One day he arrived late for class and found two problems on the blackboard. He thought these were for homework so he copied them down. A few days later he turned them in late with an apology for taking so long to get them done. Six weeks later on a Sunday morning at about 8 am, the professor knocked on George's door all excited, wanting him to sign off on a paper for publication. At first George did not know what this was all about. Since George had arrived late for that one class, he had missed the instructor's explanation that the problems on the board were not homework but two famous unsolved problems or (more accurately) unproved statistical theorems. He hadn't known the problems on the board were unsolvable. You see, if he had believed they were impossible he never would have tried to solve them. It was done by believing it could be done! Faith is powerful. But, as amazing as this is, understand that it was accomplished by having faith in self—believing self could do it.

I remember being enthralled as a kid watching the 1968 Olympics held in Mexico City. There was an American athlete named Dick Fosberry. He changed the sport of high jumping forever. He popularized and perfected what became known as the Fosberry flop. Before running towards the bar, there was a time during which he stood before an excited Olympic crowd meditating and psyching himself up for four and a half minutes. When he would jump, all eyes would be on him in the stadium filled with 80,000 spectators. He set a new Olympic record and won a gold medal by clearing seven feet, four and one-fourth inches! After his jump he said, "I guess I use positive thinking. Every time I approach the bar I keep telling myself, 'I can do it, I can do it.'" He visualized before he actualized! So faith is powerful but, once more, this was done with faith in self and not faith in God. Faith in self is powerful but is always limited, because we all know we have limits. Faith in God is always unlimited, because there are no limits with God!

## Believing Without Seeing

The third faith secret is having a God kind of faith—visualizing before actualizing.

> *Then Jesus said to the centurion, "Go! Let it be done just as you believed it would." And his servant was healed at that moment. (Matthew 8:13)*

The centurion had most certainly already heard about Jesus, and he may have even seen him touch a man to cure him, but he absolutely had never seen or heard of Jesus healing someone from a distance. He demonstrated a radical faith when he told Jesus to just say the word and his servant would be healed. Jesus was totally astonished. This man fulfilled the very definition of faith found in Hebrews 11:1: *"Faith is being sure of what we hope for and certain of what we do not see."* Man says, "Seeing is believing," or "I'll believe it when I see it," or "Show me and I'll believe." God simply says, "Believe and I'll show you!" Noah built an ark for a flood although he had never seen rain. Abraham left his home having never seen his destination. Moses gave up the treasures of Egypt without first seeing his future reward. All these were commended for their faith, for they believed without seeing. Faith is our sixth sense. It must guide our lives over and above our other senses (seeing, hearing, smelling, touching, tasting). It must especially dominate our sense of sight. After all, sight is faith's greatest enemy because it makes us so limited! The mystery of how faith works is unlocked in Romans 4:17.

> *As it is written: "I have made you a father of many nations." He is our father in the sight of God, in whom he believed — the God who gives life to the dead and calls into being things that were not. (Romans 4:17)*
>
> Or: . . . *calls into being that which does not exist. (NASB)*
>
> Or: . . . *calleth the things that are not, as though they were. (ASV)*

The end of this passage can be literally translated, *calls the things which do not exist as existing.* God calls things that do not exist as if they did exist! God calls things that are not as though they were—this is a God kind of faith! God has demonstrated for us his use of faith. First, he thinks. Then he speaks confidently about the future reality of his thoughts. This shows us that faith ***visualizes*** before it ***actualizes***. Something must be a mental reality (*"certain of what we do not see"*) before it becomes a physical reality. This is how God created the universe—how he created something from nothing. This is how man "creates" an invention. It starts as a thought, a dream, a picture in the mind before it can be touched, tasted or seen. In the same way, we must learn to specifically visualize our changed life, our changed personality, our changed sin or our changed marriage before there will be any *real* changes. I saw myself leading evangelistic Bible studies before I ever led the first one. I saw myself preaching long before I ever stepped in front of an audience. I visualized churches being planted throughout Europe long before the plantings started. These were things I longed for and spoke about before they were a reality. On top of this, I believed these things could *only* happen by the power of God.

> *I pray that the eyes of your heart may be enlightened in order that you may know the hope to which he has called you, the riches of his glorious inheritance in his holy people, and his incomparably great power for us who believe. That power is the same as the mighty strength he exerted when he raised Christ from the dead and seated him at his right hand in the heavenly realms. (Ephesians 1:18–20)*

> *And Elisha prayed, "Open his eyes, LORD, so that he may see." Then the LORD opened the servant's eyes, and he looked and saw the hills full of horses and chariots of fire all around Elisha. (2 Kings 6:17)*

> *"Don't you have a saying, 'It's still four months until harvest'? I tell you, open your eyes and look at the fields! They are ripe for harvest." (John 4:35)*

We must truly understand these scriptures! God wants us to unleash his power through faith, but we must first know with certainty that our thoughts and dreams will become a reality. We must open the eyes of our heart just as the servant's eyes were opened. We must have a God kind of faith that believes the reality of something before it is tangible in any way. It must be absolutely real for us before we can touch it, smell it, taste it, hear it or see it! We are to be just like the farmer who knows the harvest exists and speaks as though the harvest exists even though there is nothing in sight and it's four months away. When we talk, the words from our lips must speak of the absoluteness of what will exist. We must call things that are not as though they were! There must be visualization before there can be actualization.

> *Now to him who is able to do immeasurably more than all we ask or imagine, according to his power that is at work within us... (Ephesians 3:20)*

We must get specific with our thoughts and dreams, knowing with certainty that God is at work to make our "imaginings" a reality. In fact, God can do even *more* than we can imagine. You should be asking yourself a few questions at this point: Do I visualize what I want to become for God? Do I visualize what I want to accomplish in my life for the glory of God? Do I hold a picture in my mind believing, without wavering, in the future reality of it? Do I call things that are not as though they were? Do I astonish Jesus with my faith? Imagine working with God's power and wisdom believing it can be done. If we think big thoughts, have a big faith, make big plans, then God will bless us with big results. Our only limitation is the size of our faith in God. With a God kind of faith, we can accomplish anything God has promised for us to do or to become.

The Spirit of God raised Jesus from the dead and the Spirit of God was moving during the creation process in Genesis. God's Spirit correlates with God's power. As Christians, we have the Spirit of God living in us. So what does this mean for us today? It means we have the same power living inside us that raised Jesus from the dead and that created the universe (Ephesians 1:19–20; Romans 8:11; Genesis 1:1–2). Now, we can't go out and raise someone from the dead or go out and create a universe. Why? Only because we were never promised we could do those things. What we can do is everything God has promised that we as his disciples can do in his word—the Bible! As we strive to change and become more and more like Jesus, let us always remember his words in Mark 10:27, which were spoken after the rich young ruler walked away from God. At this point, it seemed an impossible situation to the apostles for the rich to be saved, but Jesus said, *"With man this is impossible, but not with God; all things are possible with God."*

## Abraham: A God Kind of Faith

*Against all hope, Abraham in hope believed and so became the father of many nations, just as it had been said to him, "So shall your offspring be." Without weakening in his faith, he faced the fact that his body was as good as dead — since he was about a hundred years old — and that Sarah's womb was also dead. Yet he did not waver through unbelief regarding the promise of God, but was strengthened in his faith and gave glory to God, being fully persuaded that God had power to do what he had promised. (Romans 4:18–21)*

Our limitation is only the size of our faith in God. We acutely understand this through the life of Abraham. He received a promise from God that through his seed all nations would be blessed. He was promised to have the number of descendants like the number of stars—uncountable! But Abraham was seventy-five years old when he received this promise, and nothing happened quickly. Although he never lost faith in God fulfilling the promise, he did take it into his own hands thinking he knew how to make it happen. The idea of impregnating Hagar, his wife's handmaiden, has led to many thousands of years of conflict and disunity in the Middle East. Thinking we know a better way than God is never good thinking! Getting impatient and taking matters into our own hands can have disastrous results. Still, twenty-four years after the promise, messengers from God came to tell Abraham and Sarah they would have a child in the following year. Abraham was now ninety-nine and Sarah was well past the age of childbearing. She laughed, thinking, "*After I am worn out and my master is old, will I now have this pleasure?*" (Genesis 18:12). And yet Isaac, the child of promise, was born the following year. This was twenty-five years after the promise was first given! How did this happen? Well, of course it was because of God, but he used Abraham to make it occur because of his God kind of faith!

Abraham faced the facts and then he faced God. In facing God, he could now not only face the facts, he could *faith* the facts! By human reasoning: not possible. By human power: not possible.

By human effort: not possible. The facts were that his body was as good as dead and that Sarah's womb was also dead. But in his mind, having a son was already a done deal. After all, it was God who had promised, and *"Is anything too hard for the Lord?"* (Genesis 18:14). So Abraham was fully persuaded that God had the power to do what he had promised. Abraham spoke of his son as a reality long before he was ever conceived. He visualized in his mind, heart and soul that his son existed long before he was born—before he was actualized in this world physically.

Some may be asking themselves questions like: Why is God not doing big things in my life? Why is God not making big changes in me? Well, do you have a God kind of faith? People's tendency is to face the facts (what they see) without being fully persuaded that God is able and has the power to do what he promised. But the word of God says we must *"live by faith, not by sight"* (2 Corinthians 5:7.) This is to be our way of life, not just a nice saying on a pretty poster.

**FACT:** Every person who strives to please God will have challenges, disappointments and troubles in this life.

**FACT:** Every person who wants to live a godly life in Jesus will be persecuted.

**FACT:** Certain sins for certain individuals are incredibly difficult to overcome. Some sins must be dealt with a person's whole life to stay victorious over them.

**FACT:** The life God calls us to live is beyond our abilities, intellect and wisdom.

**FACT:** Every congregation that wants to do something great for God will go through many difficulties and trials.

**FACT:** Every leader who wants to lead their congregation into great growth spiritually and numerically for God has to be willing to make great sacrifices in their personal lives.

Yes, we must face the facts. We can't close our eyes to the realities of what is going on around us or of what is going on inside us. We can't close our eyes on the realities of what it will take to accomplish great things for God. But once we face the facts, we must always remember to face God so we can *faith* the facts. Remember who he is, what he has done and that he has never reneged on any of his promises.

## Faith in God Is Most Powerful

Our first full-time ministry job was for a small church in Columbia, South Carolina starting in the fall of 1977. The idea was to build a campus ministry where nothing like that had ever existed. This would take a God kind of faith. The congregation was not growing. When asked about people being baptized they said it had been a long time. The baptistery was not even filled with water! Although there was a small core group of good-hearted adults who wanted something great to happen for God, most of the members were just Sunday-morning Christians—which is being no real Christian at all! There were a couple of willing, although not exactly godly, students at the beginning. The truth was, I thought I knew more than I really did. I was prideful and arrogant and did not do everything right in working with the adults. But I did know what God expected and I knew not to lower the bar or back down from that! Kay and I would go to the campus day after day, sharing and studying with people. We established evangelistic Bible studies in the dorms, sometimes starting in the rooms of non-Christians who were willing to host the study. We were being paid $14,000 with no health insurance or any other benefits. After a year, Kay was pregnant and we were looking at hospital bills and no insurance. That was a stressful time! Our two children, Summer and Kent, were born in Columbia. We lived there a little less than nine years before choosing to leave to go on the mission field. During that time almost 900 were baptized into

Christ. A small, unevangelistic, shrinking and dying church was reborn. There were times of great turmoil as the uncommitted resisted the commitment of Christ that we preached and that God expected. There were times when some worked hard to fire me. There were times I failed to say or do the right thing as my young age left me insensitive and impatient. We had our tears, our times of wanting to give up and our times of personal life struggles. But so much good was accomplished far beyond our ability through *faith in God.*

We went to Tokyo for the summer of 1986 to prepare to plant a church there. For great things to happen, we had to have a God kind of faith. We had only been to Japan one time earlier on a short visit. We did not know the language or the customs. We had not met all the others who were also on the future planting team. I remember the *Wall Street Journal* coming out at that time with a front-page article stating that Japan was the Mount Everest (their words) for effective Christian mission work. The FACTS got written up in the *Wall Street Journal*! The Japanese people had resisted anything "Christian" in their culture. But I remember setting the goal for this little team to have 100 people come to an invitation service. We not only invited a great number of people to come, we also cleaned the building and the grounds. We had enough seating and enough food prepared for 100 people. We prayed, knowing it was beyond our power and ability to do this, but we could visualize in our minds the little building being full. On a Sunday morning, in Tokyo, over 100 people came to hear the word of God being preached! This was accomplished by *faith in God!*

In May 1988 we were asked to take a small group from Boston to restart a church in Orlando, Florida. This was a historic time of bringing campus ministry groups into what had become a worldwide church-planting movement. Although the church was full of good-hearted people, a time of repentance, recommitment and renewal was desperately needed. There were many who were lukewarm, there were undealt-with sins to confront, and there was a great lacking in evangelistic zeal. We went willingly, but we also went with some fears and some insecurities, since it was the first time for us to do something quite like this. But, mainly, we went believing God could do it—that God could change it. We could see in our minds what God wanted to happen. We could see hundreds of new people coming to the first service. We could see the joy level and the commitment level of the disciples get reignited. In the end, the Orlando Church of Christ was born. This was not just a new name. It was a new spirit and a new heart. There was an evangelistic explosion that resulted in great numbers getting baptized and becoming true Christians. All of this came about because of *faith in God*.

In September 1988 Kay and I led a small group made up of Americans and a few Germans to plant a church in Munich, Germany. Our first four months would be our planternship. The church would officially be started at the beginning of 1989. This was another place of finding ourselves trying to figure it out as we trusted in God. We would do public singing to draw crowds and then preach and invite the people out to church. We did many other "wild and crazy" things to share our faith and study with people. At my core, I am a people-pleaser and fearful of what others may think about me. I was fearful and self-conscious a lot. But, after four months, many people (fourteen if my memory serves me right) had been baptized into Christ—a best up to that time in our church-planting movement for foreign language plantings. Again, God was creating something out of nothing because of a *God kind of faith*.

Because of an emergency need in Paris, we arrived there at the end of December 1988. It was Christmas time. The day we moved there was the first time we had ever been in France. We restarted the church, helping people to reembrace the correct convictions of having Jesus as their Lord and Savior. Starting with just forty members in 1989, God moved and we saw over 100 people baptized into Christ naming Jesus as their Lord the first year in this very beautiful but very sinful and atheistic city. In all these situations, I often felt fear and usually felt a deep inadequacy of being able to do what was being asked and expected. These situations called for a God kind of faith—calling things that are not as though they were—visualizing before actualizing. This is having *faith in God!*

## Not Faith in Self and Not Faith for Self

It is a sad day in the life of a church when self-oriented faith principles get thrown into the teaching and preaching of Christianity. It will motivate and stimulate for a while, but the excitement will eventually die. Only God is the giver and sustainer of life. To the extent that God is removed and replaced with self, to that extent death is brought into the church. Church growth, numerically and spiritually, can only be sustained with faith in God. Faith in self or faith in God for self means eventual death to any individual or to any congregation. Unfortunately, I have seen with my own eyes the destruction of individual lives, families and whole congregations as the result of having a self-oriented faith or selfish faith. So let me say this again...faith in self or faith in God for self means eventual spiritual death! Anything done for self becomes empty and meaningless. When Christians begin to feel the emptiness and the meaninglessness of their self-oriented Christianity, they begin to lose their hope and their joy. At that point, the devil has won a great victory. Satan always loves to take beauty or truth and twist it just enough to make it deadly! He has done this with sex, money, pleasure and possessions, and he is doing it with the power of faith. Faith in self does release a real power, and power is appealing. But faith in God unleashes the mightiest power available to man. All these powers can change a person's life, but only God's power can make us everything we were created to be, everything we deeply desire to be and everything we desperately need to be!

And so we have now learned Faith Secret 3. We must have...

**A God Kind of Faith—Visualize to Actualize.**

# FAITH SECRET 4

## Result-Measured Faith

*As Jesus went on from there, two blind men followed him, calling out, "Have mercy on us, Son of David!"*

*When he had gone indoors, the blind men came to him, and he asked them, "Do you believe that I am able to do this?"*

*"Yes, Lord," they replied.*

*Then he touched their eyes and said, "According to your faith let it be done to you"; and their sight was restored. (Matthew 9:27–30)*

The desperation that these blind men felt is obvious. They wanted to see, but just wanting something did not make it happen. They had to absolutely believe Jesus could do it! The same is true for us. We can sincerely want a changed character, but do we believe it will be done? We can sincerely want to deal with a particular sin, but do we believe it will be done? We can sincerely want to win people to Christ, but do we believe it will be done?

The goal of these two blind men was to see. Jesus told them, "*According to your faith let it be done to you.*" By saying these words we learn Faith Secret 4: Result-Measured Faith. Jesus correlated the blind men's end result to the degree of their faith. This is the same principle God uses today. According to your faith let it be done to you! Results are according to our faith. Success or lack of success in your goals or in your life is a direct measurement of your faith. When we make faith goals and do not see good results, this can actually end up hurting our faith. A person can become less expectant. An honest evaluation about the real depth of our faith is needed.

The blind men left excited about the end results of their faith. Faith in God brings results that can be measured. The greater the faith, the greater the results!

## Faith Accomplishes the Impossible

> *"Lord, have mercy on my son," he said. "He has seizures and is suffering greatly. He often falls into the fire or into the water. I brought him to your disciples, but they could not heal him."*
>
> *"You unbelieving and perverse generation," Jesus replied, "how long shall I stay with you? How long shall I put up with you? Bring the boy here to me." Jesus rebuked the demon, and it came out of the boy, and he was healed at that moment.*
>
> *Then the disciples came to Jesus in private and asked, "Why couldn't we drive it out?"*
>
> *He replied, "Because you have so little faith. Truly I tell you, if you have faith as small as a mustard seed, you can say to this mountain, 'Move from here to there,' and it will move. Nothing will be impossible for you." (Matthew 17:15–20)*

Faith accomplishes the impossible! Faith gets results! The disciples who were trying to perform this healing found themselves all alone. Jesus, along with Peter, James and John, had been on a mountain top experiencing the transfiguration. This must have been the most difficult case for healing that the rest of the apostles had ever come up against without Jesus at their side. So why was there failure? Because there was such little faith! Little faith means little results. Jesus was quite expressive of his disapproval and disappointment. Then he went on to teach that nothing will be impossible for those who believe. There will be results. This sounds great, but do we really believe it ourselves and do we really understand what is being said?

In context, we must realize that the phrase "*nothing will be impossible*" is in regard to that which had been promised to these apostles. In Matthew 10:1, Jesus promised his apostles the ability "*to drive out evil spirits and to heal every disease and sickness.*" This was a promise given to them, not to everyone. With this understanding, we can correctly apply the words of Jesus and bring it out of the ethereal realm. (Note: we shared this concept in a similar way in the last section dealing with Faith Secret 3.) Jesus never promised we could fly, jump 100 yards or run a mile in ten seconds. But do we have faith in what has been promised?

What each person must do is to go through the Bible and specifically claim God's promises for themselves. Then, nothing (none of those claimed promises) will be impossible. Unfortunately, there are far too many Christians who naively fail to claim God's promises. They become like the man who saved his money for a long time to go on a cruise. The price of the ticket took all his money, so he had none left over for food. For one week he ate the crackers and cheese that he had brought in his suitcase. On the last day of his cruise, a steward asked if there was something wrong with the ship's food. The man assured him that it was probably very good but that he could not afford it. The steward's reply was, "But, sir, you don't understand. All the food you care to eat is included in the price of the ticket!" There was plenty of food; he just didn't know it was already his. All he had to do was claim it! There are plenty of promises that make the impossible possible; we just need to go claim them as our own!

Jesus promised that with faith, we can move mountains. When a mountain moves, the result is obvious and measurable. A mountain is something specific and real and big. When something big has been moved out of the way or out of our lives, we see the result in a big way. What mountains need to be moved in your life so that you can become more like Christ? Do you need to move by faith Mount Fear, Mount Laziness, Mount Sin or Mount Pride? Do you need to move Mount Fruitlessness, Mount Discouragement, Mount Materialism, Mount Bitterness or Mount Unforgiveness? Do you need to move Mount Financial Irresponsibility, Mount Unhappy Marriage, Mount Prejudice or Mount Addiction? First, find specific promises in the Bible dealing with your "mountain." Then claim those promises as your own, being fully persuaded that God will keep his promises. And according to your faith, let it be done to you. God promises and gives results!

## Jesus Amazed

*He could not do any miracles there, except lay his hands on a few sick people and heal them. He was amazed at their lack of faith. (Mark 6:5–6)*

There are only a few times when it is recorded in the Bible that Jesus was "*amazed.*" Here he was amazed at their lack of faith. At this point in his ministry, Jesus had returned to his home town to preach and teach. At first, people were amazed at his teaching. But, instead of thinking about what was being taught and how that should be applied to their lives, they started thinking from a humanistic point of view about who Jesus was and where he had come from. This effectively killed their possible faith and possible obedience to the teachings.

How often do we do this very thing? We hear some great teaching from God's word and it begins to thrill our hearts and amaze our minds. But then we get humanistic. This usually happens as we realize what the full implications are for our own lives if we were to become obedient to the teachings we have heard. We start to question the teachings in such a way that we no longer are wrestling with the truth and with how we need to change our lives; we are only thinking about the reasons it doesn't work or fit into our way of thinking and our way of life. We begin with the rationalizations and we end with the excuses. In the final analysis, all that's left is unbelief. For Jesus, the end result was that he could not do much. Now that's what's really amazing here. Jesus, God in the flesh, could not do any miracles except some little healings. And why was this? Because of people's lack of faith! Once again we have the truth of Faith Secret 4 exposed:

result-measured faith—the end result is a direct measurement of our faith. Here there were little to no results because there was little to no faith. This is very sad. Just think what could have been done in Jesus' hometown. Just think about what Jesus wanted to do back home for his old friends and family. And it is very sad for us also when we end our thought process with all the reasons something is *not* going to work or *not* going to happen or *not* going to change. Just think of what Jesus could do and would like to do in our lives. It's a matter of the measure of our faith.

## The Fall of The Wall

In 1987, I went with several others on a mission scouting trip to Berlin, Germany. At that time, the wall between East and West Berlin was still standing. The trip was planned to discover the best way to plant new churches in the German-speaking world. I will never forget passing through the checkpoint into East Berlin. Passing through the stretch known as "no man's land," we saw the soldiers, the dogs, the machine guns and the barbed wire. We saw the guard towers and most of all we saw The Wall. We bought our East German money (required for entrance and it could not be exchanged back) and then we proceeded to walk into what seemed as "enemy territory." The actual enemy was of course Satan, as he had a death grip of atheism with no freedom of religion on that region of the world.

The contrast between East and West Berlin was remarkable. On the east side, the buildings and the overall atmosphere were gray and dreary. Over the next number of hours, we saw Russian soldiers marching in the street and various statues of Lenin. We visited a war museum and found some wild ideas about history. To say the least, the Russians were the good guys who had given freedom to Europe! As we walked the streets we asked the question of how we could ever get the gospel into East Germany and the Eastern Bloc countries to give these people the opportunity to have salvation. We came up with some of the craziest and silliest ideas. But we were serious about doing whatever it would take to get it done. We prayed on both sides of the wall for the people of Germany. We prayed for the wall to fall.

We decided the first planting would be in Munich. We believed it was the place most open to the gospel at that time. We wanted to make a special effort in converting students. They would be the ones who could move most easily and who could make an impact the fastest. The second city would be Berlin, once we had a sizable group of Germans converted to Christ. We had faith. We went to work believing God could do anything. I must confess I was more in the category of *"I do believe; help me overcome my unbelief!"* when it came to effectively evangelizing East Germany and the Eastern Bloc countries. You already know the rest of the story. Just two short years after our first trip to Berlin, in November 1989, the world party started as the wall came down. Kay and I were living in Paris at that time, but we had to join the party and see the miracle for ourselves. We flew out of Paris into West Berlin. This time we freely walked into East Berlin and we literally chipped away at the wall ourselves. I wanted to "help" knock it down! There was still much insecurity and uncertainty about the future of Berlin and of Germany and the Iron Curtain countries. The atmosphere was one of cautious optimism. But it was obvious that God was moving in our history of the world. I know that many disciples from around the world were praying for open doors for world evangelism and praying specifically for the German and Russian people. By the faith of many the wall fell. I can't explain it any other way. Soon after the fall of the wall, the church was planted in Berlin. I remember evangelizing in the streets before the first service. I also remember that some of the first converts were from East Berlin!

I have been to Jericho and have seen some of the excavated walls of that city. The Israelites were told to march around one time for each of six days and then on the seventh day to walk around it seven times blowing the rams' horns and giving a loud shout. Now, what made the wall fall? Obviously it was God! Why did the wall fall? Because the Israelites demonstrated their faith by doing exactly what God had said to do. When the walls of Jericho fell, it was a miracle of God. When the Berlin Wall fell, it was a miracle of God. Where there is faith, there are results. The bigger the faith, the bigger the results! God wants the world evangelized. He wants his message to be heard by everyone. Because this is God's will, he is working to make it happen and will always use those who have a radical faith. We are thankful for all who were on the different teams going to different countries with a radical faith in God. It was because of the faith of so many that God was able to move so powerfully. God can bring any wall down (or move any mountain) in our lives or in this world. It's just a matter of faith!

And so we have now learned Faith Secret 4: according to your faith it will be done to you. Where there is a lack of faith, there will be a lack of results.

**The greater the faith, the greater the results!**
**That's Result-Measured Faith.**

# FAITH SECRET 5

# Prayer, Fasting, Power and Faith

*Now the Lord is the Spirit, and where the Spirit of the Lord is, there is freedom. And we all, who with unveiled faces contemplate the Lord's glory, are being transformed into his image with ever-increasing glory, which comes from the Lord, who is the Spirit. (2 Corinthians 3:17–18)*

## Never Forget the Big Picture

As we go deeper into the faith secrets, we must never forget the big picture. The big picture is always Jesus. He is the one whom we are following and whom we want to be more and more like. How is this accomplished? According to the passage of Scripture above, a main key is to "contemplate" Jesus. The definition of contemplate is to *reflect on* or *muse over* or *meditate on*. The Bible has much to say about this kind or contemplation or meditation, as in these verses (all with emphasis added):

*Keep this Book of the Law always on your lips; **meditate** on it day and night, so that you may be careful to do everything written in it. Then you will be prosperous and successful. (Joshua 1:8)*

*Within your temple, O God*
*we **meditate** on your unfailing love. (Psalm 48:9)*

*I will consider all your works*
*and **meditate** on all your mighty deeds. (Psalm 77:12)*

*I **meditate** on your precepts*
*and consider your ways. (Psalm 119:15)*

*I reach out for your commands, which I love*
*that I may* ***meditate*** *on your decrees. (Psalm 119:48)*
*I have more insight than all my teachers,*
*for I* ***meditate*** *on your statutes. (Psalm 119:99)*

*My eyes stay open through the watches of the night,*
*that I may* ***meditate*** *on your promises. (Psalm 119:148)*

*I remember the days of long ago;*
*I* ***meditate*** *on all your works*
*and consider what your hands have done. (Psalm 143:5)*

*They speak of the glorious splendor of your majesty—*
*and I will* ***meditate*** *on your wonderful works. (Psalm 145:5)*

Before we talk specifically about prayer, fasting, power and faith, let's take time to weave together some of the faith secrets we have discussed so far. This will get us ready for Faith Secret 5.

Remember that faith comes by God's word—the Bible. One of our faith potentials is that the level of the word of God placed on our hearts and held in our minds constitutes how much faith we can have. As we are deliberate and consistent and deep in the study of God's word, our faith will grow.

We are also called to "visualize" becoming all of what we are called to be and doing all that we are called to do in God's word. We must remember that humility is crucial, since these things can only be accomplished by the power of God. The Bible creates the right picture in our minds. Meditation gives focus to the picture and also sustains it. And then prayer (our next subject) releases God's power to "actualize" (bring into tangible reality) this picture or dream. Our overall goal is to be like Jesus Christ. The way to be transformed into him is to contemplate, behold, reflect and picture Jesus in our minds. But watch out! If our concepts or perceptions of Jesus are not right or not complete, we will become a distorted Jesus instead of becoming like the real Jesus. Therefore, the key to transforming our personal lives is visualizing the Jesus of the Bible and, through the Spirit's power, becoming like him!

As we are looking at the big picture, let us remember that Christianity is having an intimate and dynamic relationship with God. All relationships take faith to exist. This is true for husbands and wives, this is true for parents and children and this is true of our relationship with God. Faith or trust must be at the center for there to be an established relationship. And relationships take communication. And so the Bible has much to say about prayer and faith.

## Eternal Relationship Between Prayer and Faith

> *Then Jesus told his disciples a parable to show them that they should always pray and not give up. He said: "In a certain town there was a judge who neither feared God nor cared what people thought. And there was a widow in that town who kept coming to him with the plea, 'Grant me justice against my adversary.'*
>
> *"For some time he refused. But finally he said to himself, 'Even though I don't fear God or care what people think, yet because this widow keeps bothering me, I will see that she gets justice, so that she won't eventually come and attack me!'"*
>
> *And the Lord said, "Listen to what the unjust judge says. And will not God bring about justice for his chosen ones, who cry out to him day and night? Will he keep putting them off? I tell you, he will see that they get justice, and quickly. However, when the Son of Man comes, will he find faith on the earth?" (Luke 18:1–8)*

In this parable (one we will look at again in connection with Faith Secret 7), Jesus teaches us that we are to pray and not give up. We are to have persistent prayer. Then after making the point about persistent prayer, Jesus asks the question: "*When the Son of man comes, will he find faith on the earth?*" With this connection made by Jesus, we now know that prayer and faith are eternally related and connected in the mind of God. Prayer is a demonstration of our faith. A way that we can understand the relationship more clearly is the following:

**Little Prayer = Little Faith**
**No Prayer = No Faith**
**Much Prayer = Much Faith**

Some may want to protest and say this isn't true, but it is! Jesus teaches about prayer and then asks the question about faith. The amount of prayer and the amount of faith are linked. The degree of prayer is a degree of faith, since prayer is a demonstration of our faith.

## The Tale of Two Prayers

In Luke 18:9–14 Jesus told another parable that dealt with prayer. This time the emphasis was on humility, and we should remember that one of our faith potentials is the degree of our heart's humility before God. The greater the humility, the greater the faith potential. As we will see, not all prayers move God. It is the prayer of humble faith that moves God.

> *To some who were confident of their own righteousness and looked down on everyone else, Jesus told this parable: "Two men went up to the temple to pray, one a Pharisee and the other a tax collector. The Pharisee stood by himself and prayed: 'God, I thank you that I am not like other people — robbers, evildoers, adulterers — or even like this tax collector. I fast twice a week and give a tenth of all I get.'*
>
> *"But the tax collector stood at a distance. He would not even look up to heaven, but beat his breast and said, 'God, have mercy on me, a sinner.'*
>
> *"I tell you that this man, rather than the other, went home justified before God. For all those who exalt themselves will be humbled, and those who humble themselves will be exalted."*

Although God heard the prayers of both men, only one man connected with God. Only one went home justified before him. Although through this teaching Jesus was mainly dealing with those who were self-righteous, he exposed the self-righteous heart in a story about prayer. Our hearts must be in a humble place for God to be moved by our prayers!

Let's consider for a moment Nehemiah's prayer that we have recorded for us in Nehemiah 1:6, 11.

> *"Let your ear be attentive and your eyes open to hear the prayer your servant is praying before you day and night for your servants, the people of Israel. I confess the sins we Israelites, including myself and my father's family, have committed against you. . .*
>
> *"Lord, let your ear be attentive to the prayer of this your servant and to the prayer of your servants who delight in revering your name. Give your servant success today by granting him favor in the presence of this man."*
>
> *I was cupbearer to the king.*

Nehemiah has an obvious spirit of humility as he comes before the Almighty God and makes his request. It is interesting to note that it took four months of humble prayer before God opened the door for his request to be granted. And then, Nehemiah got more than he had even imagined as God moved the heart of the king to give him the permission to go, the access to materials needed to build and even an escort on the 800-mile journey to get him safely to Jerusalem. Throughout the book of Nehemiah, we can see that he was a man of prayer. And because of his humility, God was moved to answer those prayers.

As we talk of humility and prayer, let's not forget the Gethsemane prayer. Jesus was facing the reason he had come. He knew that the plan was for him to take into his body the sins of mankind and then to die. This would cause a separation for the first time ever between the Father and the Son. And so, Jesus prays the intense, broken-capillaries-in-the-face, bloody-sweat prayer asking if there could be ANY other way to save humanity. Jesus did not want to go through the pain and separation. He expressed his will to the Father. But then he concluded the crying-out-to-God prayer with the words, "*Yet not my will, but yours be done.*" He prayed, but he would accept a "No" answer. He was humble enough to submit to the Father's plan for him. What trust! What FAITH demonstrated through this humble prayer. He was willing to do whatever God wanted him to do. And ultimately, God raised him from the dead and seated him at his right hand.

## Prayer Is the Answer

We are going to look again at the time when Jesus was coming from the Mount of Transfiguration with Peter, James and John. This event had left the rest of the apostles alone doing the work of the ministry. We have seen that all the apostles had been given the power to heal (Matthew 10:1) but now they find themselves failing with a particular case. Eventually, they ask the question of why they couldn't heal the boy. Here's the story.

*When they came to the other disciples, they saw a large crowd around them and the teachers of the law arguing with them. As soon as all the people saw Jesus, they were overwhelmed with wonder and ran to greet him.*

*"What are you arguing with them about?" he asked.*

*A man in the crowd answered, "Teacher, I brought you my son, who is possessed by a spirit that has robbed him of speech. Whenever it seizes him, it throws him to the ground. He foams at the mouth, gnashes his teeth and becomes rigid. I asked your disciples to drive out the spirit, but they could not."*

*"You unbelieving generation," Jesus replied, "how long shall I stay with you? How long shall I put up with you? Bring the boy to me."*

*So they brought him. When the spirit saw Jesus, it immediately threw the boy into a convulsion. He fell to the ground and rolled around, foaming at the mouth.*

*Jesus asked the boy's father, "How long has he been like this?"*

*"From childhood," he answered. "It has often thrown him into fire or water to kill him. But if you can do anything, take pity on us and help us."*

*"'If you can'?" said Jesus. "Everything is possible for one who believes."*
*Immediately the boy's father exclaimed, "I do believe; help me overcome my unbelief!"*

*When Jesus saw that a crowd was running to the scene, he rebuked the impure spirit. "You deaf and mute spirit," he said, "I command you, come out of him and never enter him again."*

*The spirit shrieked, convulsed him violently and came out. The boy looked so much*

> *like a corpse that many said, "He's dead." But Jesus took him by the hand and lifted him to his feet, and he stood up.*
>
> *After Jesus had gone indoors, his disciples asked him privately, "Why couldn't we drive it out?"*
>
> *He replied, "This kind can come out only by prayer." (Mark 9:14-29)*

Jesus came down from the Mount of Transfiguration feeling refreshed, but he found his refreshment short lived. A boy had been brought to his disciples to be healed, but they had failed. The boy's father was not happy about it. Jesus' response to all of this was that it was a faith problem: *"You unbelieving generation"*! Suddenly, the boy started convulsing right in front of him. The question was asked about how long he had had the problem. The answer was that it had been a long time...ever since childhood. Quite often, due to the longevity of a problem, greater doubt exists about being able to fix the situation. So the father said to Jesus...IF you can do anything. At this statement, Jesus had a strong reaction...IF I can? The "if" showed the lack of faith concealed in the heart of the father. Then Jesus goes on to say, *"Everything is possible for one who believes."* Finally the boy's father asks for help to have the kind of faith that is needed to see his son healed.

But did you catch what Jesus just said? Everything is possible for one who believes! It's a FAITH issue. It's always a faith issue! Our faith makes the possibilities in our lives come alive. Let's remember once again that the *"everything"* refers to whatever we have been promised by God to be able to do. We haven't been promised to jump 1000 feet in the air or to swim a mile in 10 seconds. But whatever we have been promised that we can do is possible if we believe!

The disciples were embarrassed, so they waited until they were alone with Jesus to ask the big *Why* question. Why couldn't we do it? Jesus gave them the answer: it's a matter of prayer. (Some manuscripts say it's a matter of prayer and fasting.) Again we see that faith and prayer go hand in hand in the mind of God. So at this time the disciples were relying on themselves to heal the boy. They had healed others in the past, so why not heal this boy now? They were thinking that they had the power. They had forgotten it was actually God who had the power, and so they forgot to pray. Imagine that. Doing the work of the ministry and forgetting to pray!

Prayer is an expression of our faith in God. It is faith becoming articulate. Prayer is finally allowing God to have his will in our life on his terms. Our prayers are the keys to accomplishing God's holy purposes here on earth. There is no substitute for prayer. It is more than something we do or say—prayer involves who we are!

## And Fasting Too?

Prayer and fasting go together like peanut butter and jelly or like Romeo and Juliet; they were made for each other. David certainly understood this as he prayed and fasted even for his enemies.

*Yet when they were ill, I put on sackcloth*
*and humbled myself with fasting.*
*When my prayers returned to me unanswered,*
*I went about mourning*
*as though for my friend or brother. (Psalm 35:13–14)*

Daniel also understood the relationship between prayer and fasting.

*So I turned to the Lord God and pleaded with him in prayer and petition, in fasting, and in sackcloth and ashes. (Daniel 9:3)*

And Paul understood it too.

*Paul and Barnabas appointed elders for them in each church and, with prayer and fasting, committed them to the Lord, in whom they had put their trust. (Acts 14:23)*

And so we see that prayer and fasting are linked together in Scripture. We also need to know that neither prayer nor fasting can be left out of our Christian lives. In the Sermon on the Mount, Jesus talks about both prayer and fasting. He introduces both subjects the same in Matthew 6:5 and Matthew 6:16. He says *WHEN* you pray, not *IF* you pray. He says *WHEN* you fast, not *IF* you fast. There is obviously the expectation to have these regularly in our lives.

Fasting means to abstain from food. It also means giving up something good for something better. Fasting is a form of mourning. It is also a God-approved means of humbling ourselves before him. So when we fast and are hungry, it reminds us that we are petitioning God about something specific. It also expresses to God how serious we are about what we are fasting about. And practically, the time we would have used in preparing and eating food can now be used for prayer. Fasting is a plea to God to listen to our cries. As it is coupled with prayer, it is a demonstration of faith with a big exclamation point. And so our faith should be expressed in prayer and, at critical times, in fasting too.

## God Kind of Faith vs Man Kind of Faith

The passage of Scripture found in Mark 11:20–24 is crucial for our understanding and defining of prayer and faith. I call this the Prayer of Faith.

> *In the morning, as they went along, they saw the fig tree withered from the roots. Peter remembered and said to Jesus, "Rabbi, look! The fig tree you cursed has withered!"*
>
> *"Have faith in God," Jesus answered. "Truly I tell you, if anyone says to this mountain, 'Go, throw yourself into the sea,' and does not doubt in their heart but believes that what they say will happen, it will be done for them. Therefore I tell you, whatever you ask for in prayer, believe that you have received it, and it will be yours."*

"*Have faith in God.*" This statement actually aligns with the Romans passage we have discussed in Romans 4:17 concerning having a God kind of faith. Let's look at Mark 11:22 in the Young's Literal Translation and in the Wycliffe Bible.

*And Jesus answering saith to them, 'Have faith of God.' (YLT)*
*And Jesus answered and said to them, Have ye the faith of God. (WYC)*

Have the faith of God, or have a God kind of faith! (That's Faith Secret 3.) Jesus is teaching that to have mountain-moving faith, a person must have a God kind of faith as opposed to a man kind of faith. Note that Jesus never literally moved a mountain into the sea. So we don't have an example or a command of this being needful, important or necessary in our service to God. I have seen mountains literally moved with the strip mining that is done in West Virginia. This process literally takes down a mountain; even man can move literal mountains. What's the result? I have never known anything great to happen spiritually just because a literal mountain gets literally moved. So what's the point? That something huge *can* be moved! We all have some huge issues in our lives that need moving. So what may seem impossible is possible; in this case, huge things, as we have mentioned before (Mount Pornography, Mount Unhappy Marriage, Mount Relationship Conflict, Mount Fruitlessness, etc.), can get moved and thrown out!

And how is this to happen? Jesus' answer is that it is by prayer. But not just any kind of prayer. A God-kind-of-faith prayer! This is opposed to a man-kind-of-faith prayer. Man says, "I'll believe it when I see it." God says, "Believe it and you'll see it!" Man says, "Show me and I'll believe you." God says, "Believe me and I'll show you!" And so Jesus tells us that for prayer to move a mountain we must believe before we receive it: *"Whatever you ask for in prayer, believe that you have received it, and it will be yours."* We must have a God kind of faith, one that calls things that are not as though they were! The reality of the answered prayer is already to exist for us as we pray to God. All things are possible, but the limit to prayer is the limit of our faith. We shut out God when we have to see before we believe. Again, let's be reminded that we are to walk by faith and not by sight (2 Corinthians 5:7).

## Power from God

So we have seen the direct relationship between prayer and faith. We now know that prayer is one of the greatest demonstrations of our faith in God. Also, we have seen that prayer is a demonstration of our heart's humility. To pray is to show a God-sufficiency. To not pray is to show self-sufficiency. This is true at all times for all people. It doesn't matter what we say or feel. A prayerless person is always a faithless person! Prayer also determines how much of God's power is at our disposal. As the persistent widow (crying out) was able to move the unjust judge to action, how much more will the persistent prayer (crying out) be able to move the One Just Judge to action? God's power gets unleashed, and this awesome power is at our disposal. And even more than that, God's power is at our disposal *quickly!*

Let's look at a passage in James 5 specifically talking about the prayer of faith. We will start in verse 13 and take portions through verse 18.

> *Is anyone among you in trouble? Let them pray. . . The prayer offered in faith will make the sick person well. . . Pray for each other so that you may be healed. The prayer of a righteous person is powerful and effective. Elijah was a human being, even as we are. He prayed earnestly that it would not rain, and it did not rain on the land for three and a half years. Again he prayed, and the heavens gave rain, and the earth produced its crops.*

The prayer offered in faith can heal. What power! The prayer offered in faith can stop and start rain when it relates to the purposes of God. What incredible power! The prayer offered in faith can move mountains. What awesome power! And it's all available to human beings. Elijah was a part of mankind just like us. Now, in the midst of all this power, let's be acutely aware of what will inhibit God's power in our lives—our lack of personal righteousness. It's the prayer of a *righteous* person, offered in faith, that is powerful and effective. The character of the one who prays sets a limit on the answer God chooses to give.

God will always answer prayer. But it is not always a "Yes" answer. It may be a "No" answer or it may be a "Not yet" answer. We also need to embrace the fact that God has given freedom of choice to all humanity. Therefore, we may pray for another person for something specific (like for them to become a Christian), but in the end, they get to choose their own way. Certainly it makes a difference to pray for others, as God is moved to specifically work in and around their lives. But again, God will not remove the freedom of choice from individuals.

Additionally, when a prayer is offered in faith by a righteous person, God will always give the person what they need, not necessarily what they want. The basic cry of our lives must be, "Use me totally to advance your cause." He will answer all other prayers of a person on the basis of this fundamental one. He will not allow the short-term prayer (asking to make something happen *now* or to give something to me *now*) to get in the way of the long-range goal—to advance the cause of Christ in the best way. So prayer is the greatest activity of humanity. It empowers us for change and for service. Our prayers show how serious we really are to accomplish God's will while we are here on this earth. Our prayers are the keys to accomplish God's holy purposes!

So now, on top of everything else we have already seen about prayer, we come to the conclusion that prayer gives us access to the unlimited power of God. For too many Christians, they are like their cell phone that needs charging. They pick up their iPhone 6 plus (or in the future their iPhone 16 plus!) to do something important, and it's dead. There's no power! And all they had to do was plug it in. Too many disciples are unplugged from the power source; they are not plugged into God through prayer. Therefore, whenever something vital, important or urgent comes up, they find themselves powerless. A prayerless life is a powerless life!

Here's a prayer by Paul recorded for us in the Bible. It talks much about this incredible power we have available to us from God.

*For this reason I kneel before the Father, from whom every family in heaven and on earth derives its name. I pray that out of his glorious riches he may strengthen you with* ***power*** *through his Spirit in your inner being, so that Christ may dwell in your hearts through faith. And I pray that you, being rooted and established in love, may have* ***power****, together with all the Lord's holy people, to grasp how wide and long and high and deep is the love of Christ, and to know this love that surpasses knowledge — that you may be filled to the measure of all the fullness of God.*

*Now to him who is able to do immeasurably more than all we ask or imagine, according to his* ***power*** *that is at work within us, to him be glory in the church and in Christ Jesus throughout all generations, for ever and ever! Amen. (Ephesian 3:14–2, emphasis added)*

## How to Pray

Have you figured out yet that having a genuine prayer life is hard work? Jesus often got up early to be alone with God (Mark 1:35). He would spend the night in prayer before big decisions (Luke 6:12–16). He was in the Garden of Gethsemane for hours agonizing in prayer to prepare himself to do God's will (Matthew 26:36). Prayer is certainly essential and, there's no getting around it, prayer is hard work. The following are a few practical things that can be done to have a genuine prayer life:

1. Jesus said (literally) to go into your closet and pray (Matthew 6:6 KJV). We need to have a quiet and personal place for prayer. It's what we do in secret, so it needs to be in a place where we can concentrate and not be disturbed.
2. Different positions help us to concentrate and to maintain the right attitude as we pray. There is nothing wrong with sitting but what about...
    a. *Standing* (remembering we are in the presence of a King!)
    b. *Kneeling* (remembering who we are and who God is!)
    c. *With outstretched arms* (remembering we are reaching out to God!)

   d. *Walking* (remembering as we see the creation around us that we are talking to the Creator!)

3. Pray through the inspired prayers in the Bible. How does one pray for long periods of time and stay focused? A great way to facilitate that is to take an inspired prayer—perhaps a Psalm. Read a line or two and then pray about what you have just read. Maybe it's an expression to or about God. Then read another line or two and pray about what you have just read as it pertains to your life. If a line does not really hit your life or your heart, just go to the next line that does. Remember that there are inspired prayers throughout the Bible, not just in the book of Psalms. In this way, a person can pray in a focused way for hours and in a way that is for sure pleasing to God!

4. Pray continually (1 Thessalonians 5:17). We are to develop our minds and our spirits in such a way that as we go through our days, we have a prayerful attitude and an ongoing conversation with God. When you need patience at the office, pray for patience right at your desk or in the conference room. When you know you are not being as loving towards a person as you should be, pray for a loving attitude even as you are talking to them. When you are nudged by the Spirit to share your faith and are feeling fearful, pray for courage.

   I can remember the first time I was in an all-night prayer devotional soon after I had been converted. Each hour there were specific topics to pray about. There were breaks and drinks available. You could walk in or out as needed. And, early in the morning, there was a breakfast all together. And then I went home exhausted and ready to sleep. The interesting thing was that as I would wake up at times with all the noise around my dorm room, my mind was automatically talking to God! I was learning to pray continually!

5. At appropriate times, stop and pray with the people you are with. When someone asks you to pray for them about something, just have a prayer at that moment with them. When a situation comes up in a conversation about a person's need, just stop and pray for that person together. As you are making life plans and decisions with your family and friends, stop and pray in the midst of the discussion.

## Go Big or Go Home!

So how about doing something big? I've always liked the phrase, "Go big or go home!" What about doing something big with what we've just discussed about prayer and faith? A number of years ago, I traveled to Paris to help the ministry there. I had flown in to preach, teach, disciple and encourage. While waiting to preach on Sunday, I found myself with much of Saturday available to me. I decided to do a prayer walk by walking the Boulevard Périphérique. This is a twenty-one-mile long highway that encircles the 2.34 million who live within the city limits of Paris. Another eight million live in the suburbs of Paris. It was an incredible nonstop seven hours of walking and praying! Although I was mainly praying for the Paris church, I had a great time praying about my life and many people in my life. It gave me time to be grateful to God for all he has done for me and around me. It was an unforgettable time!

Another big thing I have done is a thirty-day fast. As I mentioned earlier, I have actually done this at two different times. I drank water and juices but did not eat any solid foods. These two fasts were in connection with some big things I wanted to see happen in my life and in my ministry. I believe the fasts let God know my degree of seriousness and allowed me to have concentrated time and focus on what I was working on and pleading with God to make happen. By the way, one thing I learned the hard way—you don't break a long fast with pepperoni pizza!

So what would be big for you? Maybe it's a three-day fast. Maybe it's a whole day set aside for you to be with God. Maybe it's a five-mile-long prayer walk. But whatever it is, when you go big you will always remember it...and God will too!

We have come to the end of Faith Secret 5. Let's do a quick recap...

**Little Prayer (& Fasting) = Little Faith = Little Power**
**No Prayer (& Fasting) = No Faith = No Power**
**Much Prayer (& Fasting) = Much Faith = Much Power**

# FAITH SECRET 6

## Finish-Line Faith

*"Finished last" will always be better than "Did not finish," which always trumps "Did not start."* (author unknown)

Faith begins a project and sees it through to completion. We are inspired by those who finish; they are our heroes. Books are written about those who finish. We dream of projects that we complete. We celebrate when we finish. The great desire that God has placed inside of humanity is to finish; we can't be happy, fulfilled, satisfied or successful if we don't. Let's ask ourselves some questions:

1. What if Abraham had said "No" to sacrificing his son?
2. What if Noah had stopped building the ark?
3. What if Joseph had said to God, "Enough is enough"?
4. What if Moses had chosen the riches of Egypt?
5. What if Joshua had stopped at day six going around the walls of Jericho?
6. What if David had walked away from Goliath?
7. What if Daniel had just wanted to fit in and be accepted?
8. What if Nehemiah had given up building the wall on day thirty-three?
9. What if Esther had not entered the king's presence?
10. What if Mary had had an abortion?
11. What if Jesus' last words before he died were not...IT IS FINISHED?!

Finishing is what being faithful (full of faith) is all about. The reason we esteem these people in the Bible so highly is because they all finished. They may have stumbled (all except Jesus!) along the way, but they finished living out their calling and their faith. Anyone can look good at the beginning of doing something great, but it's never how you start that counts, it's how you finish. Even if you put me in a 100-meter race with Usain St. Leo Bolt, the Jamaican sprinter who is regarded as the fastest person to ever run, I would look great for the first step or two. But what really matters? It's not how good I look when I begin, it's how I look when I finish that counts.

Consider for a moment just a few of the many in the Bible who did not finish.

1. **Saul:** A man who became king but allowed his disobedience (and therefore his lack of faith) to remove him as monarch. His jealousy and competitive spirit against David left him a lonely, angry, murderous and emotionally unstable man. He did not finish.
2. **Joash:** He became king when he was seven years old. He repaired and restored the temple in an awesome way. But in the end, he betrayed a friend's son and allowed the people to worship false gods and idols. He was removed through assassination from being king. He did not finish.
3. **Judas:** Chosen to be an apostle, he walked with Jesus and heard all the teachings and saw the many miracles. But he loved money. He stole from the contribution for the poor and he betrayed Jesus for a few extra coins. In the end he felt so sorry for himself that he committed suicide. He did not finish.
4. **Demas:** As Paul was closing out his Colossians and his Philemon letters, he sent greetings from Demas and called him a fellow worker. But just a few years later as he wrote 2 Timothy, he spoke of Demas leaving them and the ministry

because he loved the world. He did not finish.

5. **Alexander the metalworker:** At one time a vibrant and committed Christian, he failed to hold on to a good conscience and ended up shipwrecking his faith. He became a person who insulted and showed such contempt for God that he was disfellowshipped from the church. He did not finish.
6. **Hymenaeus:** He started his Christianity with love and commitment. Somewhere he got caught up in some false teaching about the resurrection. He used this in such a way that it destroyed the faith of others. And so, he had to be disciplined. He did not finish.

The sixth faith secret is Finish-Line Faith. Simply put, faith begins a project and sees it through to completion. Peter had an event in his life that is a good example of someone who started with a goal by faith but failed to complete it. Let's look at it.

> *Shortly before dawn Jesus went out to them, walking on the lake. When the disciples saw him walking on the lake, they were terrified. "It's a ghost," they said, and cried out in fear.*
>
> *But Jesus immediately said to them: "Take courage! It is I. Don't be afraid."*
>
> *"Lord, if it's you," Peter replied, "tell me to come to you on the water."*
>
> *"Come," he said.*
>
> *Then Peter got down out of the boat, walked on the water and came toward Jesus. But when he saw the wind, he was afraid and, beginning to sink, cried out, "Lord, save me!"*
>
> *Immediately Jesus reached out his hand and caught him. "You of little faith," he said, "why did you doubt?"*
>
> *And when they climbed into the boat, the wind died down. Then those who were in the boat worshiped him, saying, "Truly you are the Son of God." (Matthew 14:25–33)*

The disciples saw Jesus walking on the water. They were afraid and unsure about what was happening. Jesus tried to assure them that everything was fine. Maybe he started singing either Pharrell

Williams' "Happy" song or Bobby McFerrin's, "Don't Worry, Be Happy" to move them from fear to a smile. It must have worked for Peter. He got fired up! He said, in effect, "If it's really you, Jesus...just tell me to come to you." That statement of Peter's began the faith goal. When Jesus indicated for Peter to come to him, that's exactly what Peter could do. Peter started well by getting out of the boat, but the completion, or the finish line would be when he made it all the way to Jesus.

Now let's remember who Peter is. He is Simon son of John or, as we would say his name today, Simon Johnson. He's a very regular guy, a tough guy, a rough guy. He's a fisherman. Jesus took a liking to him real fast. He even came up with a nickname for him. He called him Peter which means "rock." So in our vernacular today, he would be called Rock Johnson (the original one!). And for the moment he was forgetting that rocks don't float!

So Rocky, I mean Peter, got out of the boat and actually walked on the water! My reaction to Peter would have been, "Great...you are phenomenal! You actually walked on water for a while. What an awesome faith you have!" But Jesus reacted very differently. He said, *"You of little faith...why did you doubt?"* How do you think Peter felt after sinking? He probably felt like the guy who was told by his doctor that he had some bad news and some worse news for him. The man asked for the bad news first and the doctor proceeded to tell him he would die in twenty-four hours. He then asked the doctor what could possibly be worse than that news...and the doctor apologetically told him that he was supposed to have told him twenty-three hours ago! As with the patient, Peter was not feeling good about the news he was just given about himself. His symptoms were doubts and the diagnosis was a deadly faith-attack! Although it was not promised by Jesus that all the disciples could walk on water, Peter was the one person who was promised that he could. And with anything promised to us by God, we are given the power to do it through our faith. Peter's faith gave out and he began to sink.

Now what was the actual problem? After all, he did walk on water for some period of time. The problem was that Peter did not finish. His "project," "plan," or "promise" was to walk the distance from the boat to Jesus. That was the faith goal he set for himself. He started out great, but he failed to finish. A few good steps did not a finish make. So many Christians have many great beginnings. They have a fired-up week or month; they start to have consistent quiet times or start to share their faith every week or every day. They start to accept more involvement and leadership in the ministry. They start to embrace the greater responsibilities and pressures that come from real involvement with people. But where are these same people in six months or a year? What has really changed in their lives? What impact has really been made in the lives of others? Has there been consistency? Have they finished their project, their plan, their promise, their goal? Too many Christians end up feeling frustrated and defeated because of many great beginnings and few great finishes. Many starts with few finishes weaken a person's faith. In the mind of God, faith begins a project or has a goal and sees it through to completion.

Why don't we complete what we start? It's because we take our eyes off Jesus who is the object of our faith, the pioneer and perfecter of our faith. When we take our eyes off Jesus, we focus on ourselves and on our own limitations. We start working based on our power instead of relying on God's power. At this point we begin to pay attention to the waves of doubt which have been beating against us and we, along with our faith, start to sink. As the waves of the sea are constant, so the waves of doubt from Satan are constant. Let's look at some of them that hit all of us.

**Wave 1:** You have never done this before. It can't be done by you, so why keep trying?

**Wave 2:** You have tried in the past and failed, so why try again? Don't set yourself up for another emotional let down.

**Wave 3:** You have other more urgent needs to consider like your job, home, school, future mate and bills, bills, bills!

**Wave 4:** You deserve a break today...and tomorrow...and the next day.

**Wave 5:** You need to really think about the negative remarks you have heard about your commitment, your purity, your zeal. You need to be more practical and realistic!

**Wave 6:** Whatever Satan throws at *you*!

We must learn to consistently focus on Jesus. He is our supreme example of finish-line faith. As he was getting closer and closer to finish his race, Satan was throwing him some waves, but it would not stop him from completing his mission. Looking again in Luke 13:31–33, we are told:

> *At that time some Pharisees came to Jesus and said to him, "Leave this place and go somewhere else. Herod wants to kill you."*
>
> *He replied, "Go tell that fox, 'I will keep on driving out demons and healing people today and tomorrow, and on the third day* ***I will reach my goal.' In any case, I must press on today and tomorrow and the next day****—for surely no prophet can die outside Jerusalem!" (emphasis added).*

It is simple yet profound faith that says, "If God said it, then I believe it, and that settles it!" Without these convictions, we will find ourselves beginning the same projects, starting with the same plans, making the same promises and setting the same goals again and again. And after a while, Christianity will seem to be plastic and unreal as we make little or no progress.

Let's think about the long-term or ultimate completion of our goal for a moment. I have known people who had a good start for two years or five years or even twenty years as a disciple. They started well but did not finish well. It's a battle for faith—to the very end. I know many more who are still in the battle!

When a person becomes a Christian, they are to count the cost before making the decision. That is just an estimate, because we can't know what the specific challenges will be for our lives. So we may not know our exact future, but we are to know what we are getting into. The decision to follow Jesus can't be just an on-the-spot, emotional decision. It's to be a well-thought-out, well-studied-out, calculated decision. It is the biggest, most important decision of a person's life, and it is to be a decision made for a lifetime. In the midst of calling people to become Christians or disciples (same thing in the Bible), Jesus tells them a story about estimating the cost.

> *"Suppose one of you wants to build a tower. Won't you first sit down and estimate the cost to see if you have enough money to complete it? For if you lay the foundation and are not able to finish it, everyone who sees it will ridicule you, saying, 'This person began to build and wasn't able to finish.'" (Luke 14:28)*

God's expectation is quite clear: what you start, you must finish! Jesus compares a building project to the beginning of the Christian life. Even in the less-important decision of building a tower or house, it's still a big life decision that needs great consideration. It does no good to begin building and then to go bankrupt and stop the process. The structure just sits there. It's no good to anyone. It just represents waste: wasted time, money, effort and dreams. The person who stops building is then ridiculed. And so it is with people who enthusiastically start out their Christian lives telling friends and family that Jesus is the best thing that ever happened to them. But then sometime later, they leave Jesus and go back to their old life. To some degree those who turn their backs on Jesus get ridiculed especially by those who witnessed their excitement. But ultimately it's Jesus who gets laughed at by the world. People will say or think, "I thought you said Jesus was the greatest, most important thing for everyone in life. Must not be so great since you gave him up!" A person who begins to build his spiritual life must finish!

I have many heroes when it comes to finish-line faith. I'll just mention three. First there is David. A man who started so well and stumbled so far. The man who graduated from fighting lions and bears to fighting Goliath. The man who had a heart of gold that turned into a heart so cold. He went from encountering victory after victory to experiencing murder after adultery. He went from counting his Psalms for God's glory to counting his men for self-glory. He messed up. He messed up his life, his family, and God's people. And yet, even in the midst of all this, David kept fighting for his faith. And at the end of his life, he still wanted to do something great for God: he wanted to build a temple in Jerusalem for the glory and honor of his God. Although God said "No" because he was a warrior with blood on his hands; God said "Yes" to doing all the preparation for his son, Solomon, who actually built the temple. He got a dream, a plan, a project, a goal in the twilight of his life and he pursued it with all his heart. David didn't just finish...David finished well!

Then there's John Mark, a young man who was surrounded by strong Christians. His mother, Mary, used their home in Jerusalem as a gathering place for disciples. His uncle, Barnabas, who was a radical leader in the movement, sold his lands for the work of the gospel. Barnabas was then sent to help in the early stages of the planting of the Antioch church. It became the great mission-sending church of the first century. Barnabas also was the one to bring Paul into a setting where he could begin his missionary impact. With his uncle's background and influence, Mark was inspired to give his life to God in a radical way. Then he was given the opportunity: he was chosen to be a member on a mission team! He started out well, but at some point he decided he did not want to continue. He wanted to go home. So for a while, Mark became a "marked" man by Paul. Mark had deserted them in Pamphylia and said "No" to the work of the ministry. When the next mission trip was being planned, Paul did not want John Mark on the team. He had failed.

But he was not a quitter. Eighteen to twenty years later, at the end of Paul's life, he makes a brief but very important statement: he writes that John Mark was useful to his ministry, and that he wanted John Mark to visit him before he (Paul) was executed. After Paul's death, John Mark attached himself to Peter, and in the end, he wrote the Gospel of Mark. John Mark did not just finish...John Mark finished well!

And finally there is Paul. He had a tough past to overcome. He had a rough start to his Christianity. He went from persecutor to proclaimer. All we need to do is read his own words to know his life and to understand finish-line faith.

> *Not that I have already obtained all this, or have already arrived at my goal, but I press on to take hold of that for which Christ Jesus took hold of me...*
>
> *I press on toward the goal to win the prize for which God has called me heavenward in Christ Jesus. (Philippians 3:12, 14)*

> *Do you not know that in a race all the runners run, but only one gets the prize? Run in such a way as to get the prize. Everyone who competes in the games goes into strict training. They do it to get a crown that will not last, but we do it to get a crown that will last forever. Therefore I do not run like someone running aimlessly; I do not fight like a boxer beating the air. No, I strike a blow to my body and make it my slave so that after I have preached to others, I myself will not be disqualified for the prize. (1 Corinthians 9:24–27)*

> *I have fought the good fight, I have finished the race, I have kept the faith. (2 Timothy 4:7)*

Paul did not just finish...Paul finished well!

Years ago, I heard a poem that moved me to tears. I have since used the poem in my preaching in many parts of the world. It speaks so clearly of finish-line faith that we each need to possess. As you read it, think of the father in the poem representing our Father in heaven.

## THE RACE

By Dee Groberg (one of many versions)

The whistle blew and off they went, young hearts and hopes of fire;
To win, to be the hero there, was every boy's desire.
And one boy in particular—his dad was in the crowd—
Was running near the lead and thought, "My dad will be so proud."

But as he speeded down the field across a shallow dip,
That little boy who thought to win lost his step and slipped.
Trying hard to catch himself, his hands flew out to brace,
And mid the laughter of the crowd, he fell flat on his face.

So down he fell, and with him hope; he couldn't win it now.
Embarrassed, sad, he only wished to disappear somehow.
But as he fell, his dad stood up and showed his anxious face,
Which to the boy so clearly said, "Get up and win the race!"

He quickly rose, no damage done, a bit behind, that's all,
And ran with all his mind and might to make up for his fall.
So anxious to restore himself, to catch up and to win,
His mind went faster than his legs; he slipped and fell again.

He wished that he had quit before with only one disgrace,
"I'm hopeless as a runner now, I shouldn't try to race."
But in the laughing crowd he searched and found his father's face,
That steady look that said again, "Get up and win the race."

So he jumped up to try again, ten yards behind the last,
"If I'm going to gain those yards," he thought, "I've got to run real fast."
Exceeding everything he had, he regained eight or ten,
But trying so hard to catch the lead, he slipped and fell again.

Defeat! He lay there silently; a tear dripped from his eye,
"There's no sense trying anymore, three strikes, I'm out...why try?"
The will to rise had disappeared, all hope had fled away,
So far behind, so error prone, a loser all the way.

"I've lost, so what's the use?" he thought, "I'll lie with my disgrace."
But then he thought about his dad, who soon he'd have to face.
"Get up," an echo sounded low, "Get up and take your place.
You were not meant for failure here; get up and win the race."

With borrowed will, "Get up" it said, "you haven't lost at all,
For winning is not more than this—to rise each time you fall."
So up he rose to win once more, and with a new commit,
He resolved that win or lose, at least he wouldn't quit.

So far behind the others now, the most he'd ever been,
Still he gave it all he had and ran as though to win.
Three times he'd fallen stumbling; three times he'd rose again,
Too far behind now to hope to win, he still ran to the end.

They cheered another boy who crossed the line and won first place,
Head high and proud and happy; no falling, no disgrace.
But when the fallen youngster crossed the line, in last place,
The crowd gave him the greater cheer for finishing the race.

And even though he came in last, with head bowed low, unproud;
You would have thought he'd won the race, to listen to the crowd.
And to his dad, he sadly said, "I didn't do so well."
"To me you won," his father said, "you rose each time you fell."

Finish-line faith is needed to complete the ultimate goal, and it is needed to finish the individual faith goals that we make throughout our lives. The words of Peter (Rock Johnson!) are quite significant in light of what we have just studied. They are found in 1 Peter 1:8 (emphasis added).

*Though you have not seen him, you love him; and even though you do not see him now, you believe in him and are filled with an inexpressible and glorious joy, for you are receiving the **goal** [end result] of your faith, the salvation of your souls.*

For emphasis, let me say it again in some different words: what we must realize is that the Christian life is made up of completing many faith projects, faith plans, faith promises and faith goals throughout our lifetime as a disciple. As we complete those, we are setting ourselves up to complete the ultimate goal of our faith...to be with God in eternity!

Now we have Faith Secret 6...

**Finish-Line Faith.**

# FAITH SECRET 7

## Reasoning-with-God Faith

*Leaving that place, Jesus withdrew to the region of Tyre and Sidon. A Canaanite woman from that vicinity came to him, crying out, "Lord, Son of David, have mercy on me! My daughter is demon-possessed and suffering terribly."*

*Jesus did not answer a word. So his disciples came to him and urged him, "Send her away, for she keeps crying out after us."*

*He answered, "I was sent only to the lost sheep of Israel."*

*The woman came and knelt before him. "Lord, help me!" she said.*

*He replied, "It is not right to take the children's bread and toss it to the dogs."*

*"Yes it is, Lord," she said. "Even the dogs eat the crumbs that fall from their master's table."*

*Then Jesus said to her, "Woman, you have great faith! Your request is granted." And her daughter was healed at that moment. (Matthew 15:21–28)*

The seventh faith secret is reasoning with God. Reasoning with God in prayer is an expression of great faith, and God always rewards faith, especially great faith! This is now the second of the two times in the New Testament where Jesus commends a person for having "great faith." Certainly the unnamed Canaanite woman was persistent, but more than that, she reasoned with Jesus. Initially, no one listened to her plea. No one answered her. Then she was told "No" with a short explanation: "*I was sent only to the lost sheep of Israel.*" She then approached Jesus in a very humble manner and position as she knelt and cried out, "*Lord, help me!*" Eventually she was told "No" again with a further explanation: "*It is not right to take the children's bread and toss it to the dogs.*" At first it sounds (in English) like Jesus is being cruel and demeaning towards the woman with his use of the word "dogs." In reality, he used a word that was kind and playful.

The word he used was a word denoting puppy dogs...those adorable, cute, cuddly things that we take home with us, which we let sleep with us and that we even allow to lick our faces. Jesus did not use the wild-dog word that was often used in a derogatory manner when speaking about non-Jews.

At that point, she began to humbly reason with Jesus. This demonstrated a deep belief concerning his ability to heal her daughter. She responded to Jesus by saying, "*Yes it is, Lord. Even the dogs* (the puppy-dog word again) *eat the crumbs that fall from their master's table.*" Here she got his attention, and I think a big smile, at her direct disagreement to what he had just said and with her use of the word "dog." Jesus said, "*It is not right*" and the woman said, "*Yes, it is*"! Wow, what a response! She reasoned with Jesus that it would be right for him to heal her daughter, even though she was not a Jew. She lightheartedly agreed with what Jews usually said of non-Jews, that they were like dogs that could be treated with contempt more than with care and concern, but they would at least be able to eat the scraps or the crumbs from the table. She didn't feel insulted or get defensive. She was showing that it would be reasonable for her to receive one of those little crumbs, using the analogy and the wording that Jesus had used. Jesus did not take offense at this. In fact, he was quite impressed. She had humbly reasoned with him and so he (God in the flesh) changed his mind. Jesus went ahead and granted her request after he had first said no. Her daughter was healed at that very moment. Jesus appreciated and was moved by her expression of great faith.

## We Can Change God's Mind

Let us again remember for a moment the persistent widow of Luke 18:1–8.

> *Then Jesus told his disciples a parable to show them that they should always pray and not give up. He said: "In a certain town there was a judge who neither feared God nor*

*cared what people thought. And there was a widow in that town who kept coming to him with the plea, 'Grant me justice against my adversary.'*

*"For some time he refused. But finally he said to himself, 'Even though I don't fear God or care what people think, yet because this widow keeps bothering me, I will see that she gets justice, so that she won't eventually come and attack me!'"*

*And the Lord said, "Listen to what the unjust judge says. And will not God bring about justice for his chosen ones, who cry out to him day and night? Will he keep putting them off? I tell you, he will see that they get justice, and quickly. However, when the Son of Man comes, will he find faith on the earth?"*

As we have already seen in Faith Secret 5, we are to learn to pray and not give up, since the amount of prayer and the amount of faith correlate with each other. But there is more. We are also supposed to realize what we are to do while not giving up in our prayers. The widow went to the judge time after time and did what anyone would do with a judge: she *reasoned* her case before him. Each time she came before the judge, she must have come with different reasons why he should grant her request for justice against her adversary. The implications of this are far reaching. By reasoning with God in prayer, we can actually change his mind! We cannot change the eternal purposes of God, the eternal truths of God or the eternal promises of God, but we can change his mind on how his purposes will be accomplished.

In a small way, it's like a quarterback calling plays in a football game. (Let's go with my favorite: Tom Brady of the New England Patriots, who now has four Super Bowl victories.) As I was saying, it's like a quarterback calling plays in a football game. He has one main purpose or objective, which is to move the ball forward to score points and, therefore, win the game. Someone may reason with him, and he may change his mind and run a different play or use a different player. The thing to remember is that the quarterback never changes his mind about his ultimate purpose to score points that will win the game. God's ultimate purpose (which is no game!) is for righteousness to win over wickedness, demonstrating before the entire universe the triumphant powers of love, truth and grace. As we cry out to God (who is a just and loving God in contrast to the unjust judge) day and night for justice, let us be sure to reason with him. This demonstrates great faith.

As you think about this concept of being able to change the mind of God, please note that not everyone takes such a view. There are the following scriptures we must embrace as absolutely true but that are used by some to say God never changes his mind. In James 1:17 we read: "*Every good and perfect gift is from above, coming down from the Father of the heavenly lights, who does not change like shifting shadows.*" Malachi 3:6 states: "*I the Lord do not change. So you, the descendants of Jacob, are not destroyed.*" And Numbers 23:19 reads:

> *God is not human, that he should lie,*
> *not a human being, that he should change his mind.*
> *Does he speak and then not act?*
> *Does he promise and not fulfill?*

Again, the conclusion for some from these passages is that God will never change his mind.

The thinking continues with the idea that everything is known by God and that even if a person prays for something to change and it does, then God, who is all knowing, already knew there would be prayer and already knew the situation would change and therefore there was no real change. And so, some say, there can be no changing God's mind. More scriptures used to support such a view would be Psalm 139:3–4 and 16, which read:

> *You discern my going out and my lying down;*
> *you are familiar with all my ways.*
> *Before a word is on my tongue*
> *you, LORD, know it completely. . .*
> *Your eyes saw my unformed body;*
> *all the days ordained for me were written in your book*
> *before one of them came to be.*

I have no problem with any of these wonderful scriptures. I believe as we look at all the scriptures on the subject of prayer, we find the answer that we can influence and have an effect on God's plans. As I have said and will say again, we *can't* change God's mind on his eternal purposes, on his eternal truths or on his eternal promises, but we *can* change his mind on how his purposes will get accomplished. I admit that I don't understand all of this completely. I only know what God has revealed about it to us in his word. Certainly, God is not a liar. God is not capricious. He is a loving God, a compassionate God. And my finite mind cannot discern the infinite mind of God. I don't know all of how prayer works, but I do know it does make a difference. This conclusion is not just because of my personal experience with it, but because God has promised it. God can know the outcome and still give me freedom of choice and action. My choice and action make a difference. My prayer and pleading to him make a difference. My cries to him make a difference. So many scriptures say these very things!

That certainly does *not* mean that all I reason with God about will change according to what I think. There are many heartbreaking things that occur in our lives that from our human point of reference should not happen. We must always believe that from God's point of reference, he is doing the right thing in accordance with the eternal parameters of life that he has set. We must remember that God is love and we were created in his image. Therefore, we were given the capacity to love. Within the definition of love is choice. It would mean very little if I could order a bride online to my specifications and then could push a button at any time for her to say, "I love you, Randy." For it to be meaningful, my wife would have to possess the freedom of choice, and then the words "I love you, Randy" would be deeply meaningful and significant. And so, with our ability to love comes the freedom of choice. Then it becomes a meaningful choice for us to say, "I love you, God." He did not make us programmed robots. Unfortunately, most have chosen against their true destiny of having a right relationship with God. This makes life here on earth at times confusing, challenging and painful. People's bad or evil choices can cause things to happen to others that are horrible, devastating and deplorable. Ultimately, this should lead us to the conclusion that doing right is better than doing wrong. It should also lead us to the conclusion that God does know what is best and that we need to give our lives to him.

In Genesis 18:23–33, Abraham was a man who reasoned with God in prayer.

> *Then Abraham approached him and said: "Will you sweep away the righteous with the wicked? What if there are fifty righteous people in the city? Will you really sweep it away and not spare the place for the sake of the fifty righteous people in it? Far be it from you to do such a thing — to kill the righteous with the wicked, treating the righteous and the wicked alike. Far be it from you! Will not the Judge of all the earth do right?"*
>
> *The LORD said, "If I find fifty righteous people in the city of Sodom, I will spare the whole place for their sake."*
>
> *Then Abraham spoke up again: "Now that I have been so bold as to speak to the Lord, though I am nothing but dust and ashes, what if the number of the righteous is five less than fifty? Will you destroy the whole city for lack of five people?"*
>
> *"If I find forty-five there," he said, "I will not destroy it."*
>
> *Once again he spoke to him, "What if only forty are found there?"*
>
> *He said, "For the sake of forty, I will not do it."*
>
> *Then he said, "May the Lord not be angry, but let me speak. What if only thirty can be found there?"*
>
> *He answered, "I will not do it if I find thirty there."*
>
> *Abraham said, "Now that I have been so bold as to speak to the Lord, what if only twenty can be found there?"*
>
> *He said, "For the sake of twenty, I will not destroy it."*
>
> *Then he said, "May the Lord not be angry, but let me speak just once more. What if only ten can be found there?"*
>
> *He answered, "For the sake of ten, I will not destroy it."*
>
> *When the LORD had finished speaking with Abraham, he left, and Abraham returned home.*

What an incredible example of reasoning with God. Here Abraham had a faith issue that needed to be worked out in his heart.

God had said he would destroy the wicked cities of Sodom and Gomorrah. Abraham was struggling with the concept of a loving God destroying so many that might include those who are righteous. On top of this, I'm sure he was thinking (probably with a good dose of sentimentality) about his nephew, Lot, and his family who had chosen to make their home there. Obviously that had been an unwise spiritual decision by Lot for himself and for his family. So now, Abraham began to reason with God. And notice how humble he was as he approached God. Look at his words carefully: *"Now that I have been so bold as to speak to the Lord, though I am nothing but dust and ashes... May the Lord not be angry, but let me speak just once more."* We must not think we are telling God what to do or come across as if we know what is ultimately best and ultimately right. But we can come before God with our questions and our reasoning and make our appeals to God as we see and understand them. God wants to hear what we are thinking and what we are feeling!

In this one prayer, Abraham reasoned with God numerous times. He began by getting agreement from God not to destroy the cities for the sake of fifty righteous people. Then he reduced it from fifty to forty-five righteous persons. Then from forty-five to forty. And from forty to thirty...from thirty to twenty...and finally from twenty to ten righteous persons. WOW...that's incredible! Now, you may say that the outcome was still the same, and that would be true. Yes, God knew that there were not even ten righteous people living there. The cities were still destroyed, but what wasn't destroyed was Abraham's faith. He had reasoned with God and experienced God changing his mind. And so, now knowing that God was both just and reasonable, Abraham was enabled to move forward and become known as the father of the faithful (Romans 4:11–12) and a friend of God (James 2:23).

Another wonderful example of reasoning with God is found in Exodus 32:11–14, with Moses.

> *"I have seen these people," the LORD said to Moses, "and they are a stiff-necked people. Now leave me alone so that my anger may burn against them and that I may destroy them. Then I will make you into a great nation."*
>
> *But Moses sought the favor of the LORD his God. "LORD," he said, "why should your anger burn against your people, whom you brought out of Egypt with great power and a mighty hand? Why should the Egyptians say, 'It was with evil intent that he brought them out, to kill them in the mountains and to wipe them off the face of the earth'? Turn from your fierce anger; relent and do not bring disaster on your people. Remember your servants Abraham, Isaac and Israel, to whom you swore by your own self: 'I will make your descendants as numerous as the stars in the sky and I will give your descendants all this land I promised them, and it will be their inheritance forever.'" Then the LORD relented and did not bring on his people the disaster he had threatened.*
>
> Or in the NASB: *"So the LORD changed His mind about the harm which He said He would do to His people."*
> In the NRSV: *"And the LORD changed his mind about the disaster that he planned to bring on his people."*

Here was a time in the history of Israel when God's people were incredibly disobedient. Moses was on Mount Sinai receiving the Ten Commandments. He had left his brother, Aaron, in charge of God's people. While Moses was gone, the people became fearful and felt they needed to see a tangible god in the form of an idol. And so Aaron commissioned the golden calf and the people bowed down to it and sacrificed to it. The people had been quick to become corrupt and turn from God's commandments. They were now saying that these were their gods who had brought them out of Egypt!

To say the least, God was upset. In his righteous anger he proposed to Moses a do-over. He would destroy all these disobedient people and start with Moses to raise up a people that he could use historically to bring about his eternal purposes. But instead, Moses reasons with God.

**Reason 1:** You just brought these people powerfully out of Egypt. Surely, God, you don't want to waste all that incredible effort of the plagues and the parting of the Red Sea!

**Reason 2:** The Egyptians could say that you had brought out your people for an evil purpose. The conclusion would be that you are an unloving and unmerciful God. Certainly this is not the conclusion you want people to have about the exodus from Egypt.

**Reason 3:** Don't you need to remember your promise to Abraham, Isaac and Jacob about their descendants to be as numerous as the stars? After all, you have never failed on any of your promises, and you have such a great start with the million (give or take) descendants who are here right now.

**Reason 4:** And let's not forget your promise to Abraham, Isaac and Jacob about the Promised Land. What a time it will be to see that fulfilled!

Let's remember that this was done with great humility before God. I am sure that in spirit and in speech, Moses did this right. After all, as Numbers 12:3 says, he was the most humble man on the earth at that time! (It is interesting to note that with Reason 3 and Reason 4, God would still have fulfilled those promises starting over with Moses, since Moses was a descendent of Abraham.) Let me stress again that true humility is the key to the prayer of reason. We are not telling God what to do as if we knew better. We are expressing our outlook and giving reasons to back up our thinking. To take the time and put forth the effort of reasoning our heart's desires and dreams demonstrates how deeply we believe God has the power and the love to act on our requests.

In 2 Kings 20:1–6 is still another example of reasoning with God:

*In those days Hezekiah became ill and was at the point of death. The prophet Isaiah son of Amoz went to him and said, "This is what the LORD says: Put your house in order, because you are going to die; you will not recover."*

*Hezekiah turned his face to the wall and prayed to the LORD, "Remember, LORD, how I have walked before you faithfully and with wholehearted devotion and have done what is good in your eyes." And Hezekiah wept bitterly.*

*Before Isaiah had left the middle court, the word of the LORD came to him: "Go back and tell Hezekiah, the ruler of my people, 'This is what the LORD, the God of your father David, says: I have heard your prayer and seen your tears; I will heal you. On the third day from now you will go up to the temple of the LORD. I will add fifteen years to your life.'"*

What an amazing event! The prophet Isaiah came to King Hezekiah and told him in no uncertain terms that there was no possibility for recovery from his illness. Isaiah told him to put his affairs in order because he was going to die. But Hezekiah didn't want to die yet, so he prayed to God. He reasoned with God and said he had been faithful with a wholehearted devotion. He went on and elaborated about the good he had done in his service to God. His prayer was full of pleading and emotion. And most likely, as with many places in the Bible, all of what was said or prayed is not recorded for us. But obviously, it was effective. Isaiah didn't even get out of the king's palace before God changed Isaiah's direction. Instead of leaving, the prophet of God did a 180-degree turn and went back to Hezekiah and gave him a completely different message. Isaiah told him God had heard his prayer and had seen his tears and that God would heal him. In the end, God gave him fifteen extra years to live. What a change of mind!

Again, not everything we reason with God in prayer will change. There are no simple or easy answers for when a loved one dies tragically and, to us, needlessly. Things like that are far beyond our understanding. When our best reasoning with God didn't produce the result we desired, it doesn't mean that we didn't pray well enough or often enough. Remember that God does see things from an eternal perspective that we cannot see or comprehend. Also we must remember that God did not make us robots to be controlled and manipulated. There are bad things that happen in this world that push us to our emotional limits. Ultimately, God wants to use these kinds of things to strengthen our faith, not to hurt our faith.

There was a time in David's life when he pleaded with God for the life of his baby. This was after his sin with Bathsheba was exposed by Nathan the prophet. He was told that as a consequence to his sin, the baby would die. Admittedly, this is hard for us to fully comprehend. This is found in 2 Samuel 12:15–18, 20, 22–23.

> *After Nathan had gone home, the LORD struck the child that Uriah's wife had borne to David, and he became ill. David pleaded with God for the child. He fasted and spent the nights lying in sackcloth on the ground. The elders of his household stood beside him to get him up from the ground, but he refused, and he would not eat any food with them.*
>
> *On the seventh day the child died...*
>
> *Then David got up from the ground. After he had washed, put on lotions and changed his clothes, he went into the house of the LORD and worshiped. Then he went to his own house, and at his request they served him food, and he ate...*
>
> *He answered, "While the child was still alive, I fasted and wept. I thought, 'Who knows? The LORD may be gracious to me and let the child live.' But now that he is dead, why should I go on fasting? Can I bring him back again? I will go to him, but he will not return to me."*

David pleaded; he fasted; he reasoned. He thought that God might choose to be gracious to him in this situation. In the end, the child died. David was heartbroken, but he still went and worshiped God. Since this particular event was a direct consequence of David's sin, we (from a human point of view) may find it "unfair." But God had his reasons, and even David recognized that. His surrender to the tragic event revealed that he trusted in God's eternal plan and still maintained his conviction that God was compassionate and merciful.

## Answered Prayers

As a quick refresher, remember we said in Faith Secret 5 that God always answers prayer. He may say "Yes." He may say "No." Or, he may say "Not yet." But he always answers our prayers!

As a young, eighteen-year-old disciple beginning my sophomore year in college, I started seriously praying to God for an awesome Christian wife. More specifically, I prayed to get married at the time I would graduate from college, which was less than three years away. With this prayer, I knew I would have to confront my pride and insecurities and start initiating a lot more dates, considering the fact that I had no particular interest in anyone and no one had any particular interest in me.

I reasoned with God about needing to find someone who could work with me in the ministry. I reasoned with him about the wisdom of going into the full-time ministry already married. Most of the time, I was simply sharing with God my longings and desires to have a beautiful, spiritual woman who would love me, share my dreams and make life more of a joy. I reasoned that this would help me serve him better and that it would fulfill his promise of meeting not only my needs but the desires of my heart. On Christmas day, 1976, I was on South Beach in Miami Beach reading the following poem I had written for Kay. It won't win any awards, but it made me a winner on that day. I had entitled it "The Proposal."

**THE PROPOSAL**

I couldn't love, although I tried—
I got just hurt and pain.
I couldn't love, and so I cried,
But still no true love came.

For I was lost, though now I'm found;
God rules my every part.

For He was there without a sound
And opened up my heart.

Time has passed, my love is strong—
You are a part of me.
I've loved you true, I've loved you long—
I want our love to be.

I've prayed for one, just one for life—
I know God gave me you.
So now I ask, "Will you be my wife?"
And make my dreams come true?

Kay...will you marry me?

By the way, she did say "Yes" (after being convinced that it was a real proposal and not just a poem!). Then on June 3, 1977, a few days after my last final exam of my senior year of college, God also answered with a "Yes" as we were married.

After being in the ministry for seven years, I was going through a time when I was not abundantly fruitful. I started reasoning with God. On one day I would "remind" him that people were lost and that he wanted them saved. I asked him to please let me bear much fruit. The next day I would share about the people my wife and I were meeting and how they were hurting in this or that way. I also expressed that I needed to be an example of fruitfulness to my congregation. I kept asking him to let me bear much fruit. On other days I would share with God that we needed disciples to continue evangelizing the neighborhood and city I was about to leave, having decided to do mission work in Tokyo. My consistent plea was to let me bear much fruit. In the next year, eleven people were baptized into Christ from our evangelistic Bible study (Bible Talk). Eight of those people were ones we personally had met and studied with. Most were from our neighborhood. Humble reasoning with God moves him into action. God answered this prayer with a definite "Yes"!

After living in Europe for two years, I was confronted with the possibility of a move—from leading the Paris Church to leading the Boston Church. In prayer, I had many good reasons for staying in Paris. Besides the fact that I loved the city and the people, I expressed to God that I had made many sacrifices to be there, having sold almost everything we owned. I reminded God that he had put mission work on my heart, as I had been convinced it was the greatest need of the hour. I spoke about losing developed relationships that had taken much time and effort to form. I said that it would mean another move for the kids, and that surely would not be good for them. I asked the question, "Why change the leadership here in Paris when the ministry was going so well?" I thought these were awesome reasons, but God answered with a "No."

With the perspective of being able to look back on it, I see that some of my "good" reasons were selfish in orientation. I thank God for knowing what is best. The greater challenge in Boston produced greater growth in me. Having the Boston Church for thirteen and a half years as a home base allowed much to be done for the evangelization of Europe as we planted churches from Boston throughout Europe. In addition, it gave us a financial base for the expansion of the mission field that we were asked to lead and develop. There was also a bond in the leadership group that was refreshing and absolutely needed for my spiritual well-being and for the spiritual well-being of my family. There were many challenges and many demands during those years, but I loved being there (except for the cold weather!). I loved doing what I was doing with missions and I loved all the wonderful Christians in the church. On top of all that, we saw the Boston Church grow from 3000 to 4000 disciples. We were also able to launch and finance a Christian publishing house (Discipleship Publications International). This had a tremendous impact in helping disciples around the world to have resources to grow and mature. So, God is "reasonable," but he may have the better reasons to answer a prayer with a "No."

My children, Summer and Kent, are now in their thirties, married to Christians and each have two kids of their own. My oldest grandchild is already eleven! Ever since my children's births, there were countless prayers for them: "God, please help Summer and Kent to become disciples, to marry disciples and to raise a family of disciples. Help them to love you with all their hearts for all their lives. Help Kay and me to be the parents we need to be to help them along the way." As you can imagine, with this prayer there were many reasons humbly shared with God about them becoming Christians. One of those many reasons was to keep them from the pain and the scars that follow when saying "Yes" to the different sins that come into our lives the longer we choose to live for the world. Both of my children became disciples early in life. As I have reminded them many times, they were not only saved from the sins they had committed but they were also saved from the consequences of sins they had never committed! God answered our reasoning with a "Yes."

In the past seven and a half years we have lived in Northern Virginia where we serve in the Northern Virginia Church of Christ. I am very thankful for this church and very proud of every member. I am honored to be an elder and the lead evangelist, and Kay serves as the leader of the women's ministry for the church. After being out of the full-time ministry for three and a half years, we were looking forward to again being able to focus and help many people to have a real relationship with God. Since we were coming to a church that had not been moving forward for a number of years, we wanted to help instill faith again that large numbers of people could be converted. That was one of the many reasons given in asking God to help us be fruitful. We especially reasoned with God for us to be fruitful with the older married Christians, since that is what we were ourselves. Other reasons given to God were that we needed to set an example for the church and share the joy of seeing people of our generation becoming true disciples. As it has turned out, we have now seen fifteen adults baptized into Christ and one restored from just the little house church we lead. This includes four who are in their forties and nine who are in their fifties. I believe this helped to spur the church to grow from 140 to 440 disciples during these same years as people have been baptized into Christ almost every week. And so this is another example of a reasoning prayer being answered with a "Yes."

I don't want to leave the impression that all goes well and is simple and easy if you reason with God in prayer. It certainly hasn't been for me in my Christian life. I could give examples of reasoning with God in prayer when the "No" answer was painful and difficult to accept. Probably the most challenging situation for parents occurs when their children are not spiritually receptive to God's word. As I have said before, with prayer God listens and acts, but he allows each person to make their own decisions. Children do get to decide for themselves. Of course, no parent ever gives up on their kids, so they keep on praying. And ultimately, since we can't make decisions for others, the best way to influence those around us (including our kids) is to make the right decisions for ourselves. God has an awesome plan for us. Let's be sure to keep choosing to live out his plan as we show those around us how great it is to live God's way!

As we close this chapter, here is a prayer of David's found in Psalm 13:1–6. He was a man who humbly cried out and reasoned with his God. He was a man who demonstrated great faith.

*How long, LORD? Will you forget me forever?*
*How long will you hide your face from me?*
*How long must I wrestle with my thoughts*
*and day after day have sorrow in my heart?*
*How long will my enemy triumph over me?*
*Look on me and answer, LORD my God.*
*Give light to my eyes, or I will sleep in death,*
*and my enemy will say, "I have overcome him,"*

*and my foes will rejoice when I fall.*
*But I trust in your unfailing love;*
*my heart rejoices in your salvation.*
*I will sing the LORD's praise,*
*for he has been good to me.*

Now we have Faith Secret 7...

**Reasoning with God.**

# FAITH SECRET 8

# Mission Faith

*It is written: "I believed; therefore I have spoken." Since we have that same spirit of faith, we also believe and therefore speak, because we know that the one who raised the Lord Jesus from the dead will also raise us with Jesus and present us with you to himself. (2 Corinthians 4:13–14)*

The eighth faith secret concerns what I call mission faith. We believe and therefore we speak! According to this passage, speaking about Jesus is the natural outcome of believing in Jesus. Therefore, speaking about Jesus is a defined action of faith. As our speaking goes, so goes our faith.

**Speaking = Faith**
**No Speaking = No Faith**

Speaking shows we really believe that Jesus is the Son of God. It shows we believe in heaven and in the judgment to come. It shows we believe that this world and its desires pass away, but the one who does the will of God lives forever. Our personal faith is proved genuine and has real substance only as we are personally involved in the mission of Jesus. We are all called to "fish" for men and women.

*"Come, follow me," Jesus said, "and I will send you out to fish for people." (Mark 1:17)*

*Then Jesus came to them and said, "All authority in heaven and on earth has been given to me. Therefore go and make disciples of all nations, baptizing them in the name of the Father and of the Son and of the Holy Spirit." (Matthew 28:18–19)*

"Go and make disciples of all nations." These are the marching orders from Jesus to his followers for all time—whether in the first century, the fifteenth century or in the twenty-first century. With our new life in Christ comes our new mission in life. We are to make disciples of Jesus and baptize them for the forgiveness of their sins (Acts 2:38).

## Motive to Speak

The motive behind speaking is love for God. As it says in 2 Corinthians 5:14, we are compelled by the love of Christ. In John 14, Jesus repeats himself several times, saying in various ways that if we love him, we will keep his commands. So we obey the "go and make disciples" command because we love Jesus. Our motive for speaking is also love for people. When Jesus was preaching and healing, we are told in Matthew 9:36 that when he saw the crowds, he was moved with compassion because they were harassed, helpless, directionless and unprotected. If we were to break open the heart of Jesus, we would find a heart of love for the lost. If we were to break open the heart of a disciple, we would also need to find a heart of love for the lost.

## Lifestyle Speaking

Jesus set us the example of "lifestyle speaking." He would speak about God when he went to the lake or went to the temple or went walking down a road. He would speak about God at a dinner party, when he visited a friend, when he went to a funeral. He even would speak about God at the water fountain! (in that day it was a well). The truth is, when it comes to sharing your faith, it doesn't take more time; it only takes more heart. If the gospel is actually "good news" for you, you will naturally share it. When something is great, you naturally talk about it. It could be about a movie, a restaurant, a travel destination or a particular doctor. You tell people they should go and check it out for themselves. And if Jesus is your great news, you will tell people they should go and check him out for themselves! It's on your lips because it's in your heart. Speaking out about Jesus is not what you do, it's who you are because of whose you are.

## Fruit and Faith

Being fruitful is being faithful. Being faithful is being fruitful. There is an expectation that Jesus has for all his followers to bear fruit. Not every disciple will bear the same amount of fruit, but all disciples will bear fruit.

> *"Others, like seed sown on good soil, hear the word, accept it, and produce a crop — some thirty, some sixty, some a hundred times what was sown." (Mark 4:20)*

> *"This is to my Father's glory, that you bear much fruit, showing yourselves to be my disciples. . .*
>
> *"You did not choose me, but I chose you and appointed you so that you might go and bear fruit — fruit that will last." (John 15:8, 16a)*

What does fruit mean for a disciple? Fruit would include the fruit of the Spirit, which we find in Galatians 5:22–23. Qualities like love, joy and patience would definitely be fruit. This fruit is the result of a Christian becoming more like Jesus. Fruit is also helping other Christians to become more like Jesus, and fruit is bringing others to Christ. But notice the phrase in John 15:16—"*go and bear fruit*" is just like the phrase "*go and make disciples.*" This particular sentence concerning fruit is absolutely about bringing others to Christ. Now with all this fruit, we cannot produce it or make it ourselves. It is the outcome of our attachment to Jesus, and we are attached by faith, therefore all fruit is an outcome of our faith. I teach my congregation that every time a person is baptized into Christ and becomes a Christian, everyone is being fruitful. Why? Because everyone has supported the work of this ministry with their money and everyone has been a part of the love in the church that helped draw the person to God. This does not take away from the need of every Christian to be personally involved in the mission. To be fruitful, we must demonstrate our faith by doing exactly what Jesus specifies for us to do. We don't produce fruit, but God produces fruit in us and through us because we have demonstrated our faith by being obedient to his word. God has always worked this way.

For example, consider again the walls of Jericho. What made the walls fall? Was it just faith that made it fall? Well, not exactly. Was it the shaking of the earth caused by the marching of all the soldiers that made the walls fall? Of course not. It was God who made the walls fall! But why did he do it? Because they demonstrated their faith by doing *exactly* what he said to do. All the armed men marched around the wall of the city one time for six days while seven priests carried trumpets of rams' horns in front of the ark. And on the seventh day the armed men marched around it seven times while priests were blowing the rams' horns. Then when they sounded a long blast on the trumpets the whole army gave a loud shout and the city wall of Jericho collapsed. And so the walls did fall by faith only in the sense that faith moved God into action (Joshua 6).

What healed the Aramean army commander Naaman of his leprosy? Was it just his faith? Again, not exactly. Was it the special healing H2O of the Jordan River? No. It was God who cleansed him of his leprosy! But why? Because he demonstrated his faith by doing exactly what God told him to do. He went down to the Jordan River and dipped seven times. When he came up on the seventh time, he was healed as God said he would be. And so he was healed by faith only in the sense that faith moved God into action (2 Kings 5:1–14).

Many wonder why they are not fruitful with their personal evangelism. The following seven Mission Faith Steps, correlating to the seven days of the Jericho march and Naaman's seven dips in the Jordan River, are crucial in order to develop mission fruitfulness. (I arbitrarily chose to use *seven* steps to correlate to Naaman and

Joshua—I could have broken it down differently.) To be fruitful, *all seven* Mission Faith Steps are necessary, because this is what God has specifically told us to do to be fruitful. It's a God-ordained process.

## Mission Faith Step 1: Believe the Harvest Is Plentiful

We must believe Jesus with a "God kind of faith" when he tells us the harvest is plentiful wherever we live. Some places are more open to the gospel than others, but all places are ready for a harvest of souls. If we have believed the lie that our campus or neighborhood or city or country is not open, we will not obey all the Mission Faith Steps that God gives us. As we do what God says to do, he will lead us to people searching for him.

## Mission Faith Step 2: Pray

With prayer, we are demonstrating our dependence on God and not on ourselves to produce fruit. The Bible talks about praying to be effective and praying to be bold. It's God who gives the increase.

## Mission Faith Step 3: Be a Hard Worker

The Bible teaches that we must be like the hard-working servant and the hard-working farmer. We must have the willingness to be a hard worker and not be hardly a worker. Speaking about God should be our lifestyle. To be consistent, it takes directed and focused effort. It's important to understand that there are different seasons of life. For example, there is the teen season or the campus season of life. There is the single season or the married with young kids or married with teens or empty nest season of life. There are also seasons of sickness, grief, financial hardship or prosperity.

And because of these different seasons in our lives, there will be different amounts of time available that we can give for helping non-Christians become Christians. But there can never be a season of life when we have no time for speaking about our faith. All seasons call for hard work. Some of the hard work may be in restructuring your life so there is time to do what God commands about the mission. You have to figure out your own situation determining how you can be effective in whatever season of life you find yourself in.

## Mission Faith Step 4: Scatter Seed

The seed is the word of God. It produces faith. We will not be fruitful just scattering invitations. Please don't misunderstand me; invitations are great, because they allow us to get people to church or to a small group Bible discussion. And when they come, the Word will be presented and will get placed upon their heart. But again, it is the word of God that must get scattered into many hearts. The word "scatter" depicts a lot of the Word going out indiscriminately. It is not describing just placing a few seeds in a field. So to be fruitful, we must get the word of God out upon many hearts. This is not humanistic work, it is faith work. Yes, we have to talk to many people to find the few who are wanting a right relationship with God. But because God told us to do it, it's a faith activity and not a humanistic activity. Although seemingly similar to selling such things as insurance (talk to enough people and you will sell it to some) which is *man at work*, sharing our faith is a faith activity knowing *God is at work*.

## Mission Faith Step 5: Find a Worthy Person

Jesus directed his disciples to find a worthy person and to stick with him. In the first century, that meant to stay at his home

(Matthew 10; Luke 10). A good working definition of a worthy person (sometimes called an open person) is someone who knows what you are all about, wants a relationship with you and wants to learn from you about God and his word. It describes a person who opens up their life and is willing to put forth time and effort in seeking God. It is not just a person who is open to a relationship with you. Many people want a friend. Too often, Christians are not fruitful because they are putting the precious little time they have into people who are not "*worthy*" of it. Everyone has only so much time to give to others. We must make sure we are giving our time to the right people.

## Mission Faith Step 6:<br>Be Willing to Move On

When Jesus sent out the twelve and the seventy-two disciples, he told them that they may have to, at some point, move out and move on. If the person they thought to be worthy did not actually turn out to be, they were to "*shake the dust off [their] feet.*" As we teach people the Bible, there will be some who are not willing to take it seriously by making changes or by giving the study their time and attention. When that happens, Jesus says it's time to move on. There are some who continue with people long past the time when it's clear that they are not really open to the message. It is not an unloving thing to give your time to someone else. Jesus told his disciples to take their "*peace*" back if whom they gave it to became undeserving of it. When this is done, the relationship is not going to continue at the same intensity of time, effort and initiative. Again, it's just that we all only have a certain amount of time to devote to others, and so it needs to be spent with those who show a response to the word of God. I have studied with a good number of people for four months or nine months or even a year before they became disciples. But these were people who continued to come to church and continued to give time consistently to study the Bible as life issues were dealt with and discussed.

## Mission Faith Step 7: Practice Makes Better

To be mature as a Christian, a person must become an effective teacher of the elementary truths of God's word. The only way to do that is with practice. Practice may not make us perfect but practice will always make us better. Although there are many qualities a person must grow into to be mature in Christ, one that is defined for us in the Bible is being an effective teacher. Let's look at Hebrews 5:12 and 6:1–2.

> *In fact, though by this time you ought to be teachers, you need someone to teach you the elementary truths of God's word all over again. You need milk, not solid food!...*
>
> *Therefore let us leave the elementary teachings about Christ and go on to maturity, not laying again the foundation of repentance from acts that lead to death, and of faith in God, instruction about baptisms, the laying on of hands, the resurrection of the dead, and eternal judgment.*

The passage is not talking about everyone becoming a public teacher; it is talking about everyone becoming a *personal* teacher. Therefore, a person cannot call themselves a mature Christian without being able to effectively teach others the elementary truths of Christianity.

**Maturity in the Faith = Teacher of the Faith**

This only happens when we put into practice studying the Bible with people. The more we practice, the better we get!

## Categories of Competency

How can you know your own level of competency when it comes to mission faith? Below I've listed four categories that can help you discern your present competency. As we mature in Christ, all should grow into being *Confident Studiers*. And for a congregation to sustain growth numerically, there must consistently be an increase of individual disciples who excel in their mission faith and become *Converters*. Each category assumes the incorporation of the listed specifics as you move to the next category. When we get to Faith Secret 10 about Increasing Faith, these categories will help you develop some faith goals for your own life in the area of mission faith.

**Category 1: Concerned but Unmoved**

- Knows what is right.
- Desires what is right.
- Doesn't get around to doing what is right due to fear, unbelief, laziness or selfishness.
- Needs repentance and faith.

**Category 2: Consistent Evangelizer**

- Come and see!
- Jesus has changed my life!
- Brings people to church and introduces them to others who can help study with them.
- These people at this level are awesome as they eagerly invite and share their lives.

**Category 3: Confident Studier**

- Builds a solid friendship.
- Can effectively teach the basic studies (Word of God, Discipleship, Sin, Repentance, Baptism, Church, Cross) with confidence. The right knowledge is transferred.
- Not afraid to confront people's lives with Scripture and so brings people to Christ.

- Every Christian needs to grow to this level of mission faith competency.

**Category 4: Converter**

- Expertly moves the heart with Scriptures and talks. Is able to jump into studies to help move people forward and is able to give great direction to others to help bring people all the way to Christ.
- With much wisdom and love, figures out a person's main life issues and calls for deep repentance.
- Inspires, conveys urgency and calls for a decision with sensitivity and expectation.
- Although not a level for all Christians to attain, people are desperately needed to excel to this level to sustain growth in a congregation.

Please remember the main thrust we are making with this Faith Secret. This is not primarily a chapter on how to evangelize. If it were, there would be many more scriptures and practicals that could be shared. It is a chapter about how faith works in our evangelism. We are discussing mission faith. And for us to work by faith, we need to demonstrate our faith by our obedience in doing what God teaches on how to be fruitful. Then he can powerfully work through us. God does not need men and women of great beauty or men and women of great intellect or men and women of great eloquence. God needs men and women of great faith—a radical faith that speaks out for Jesus!

The heart of God is that every generation of the world has an opportunity to hear the good news of Jesus. The strategy that we are called to for world evangelism is to go to all nations. The strategy would call to plant strong, growing churches in all the mega cities, then in all the major cities, then in every city, village, hamlet and tribe of the world. To do this, God needs people with mission faith to *stay* at home and God needs people with mission faith to *go* from home. But whether we are helping to "plant" a church or helping to "water" a church and whether we are at home or away from home, it is God who will make it grow (1 Corinthians 3:7).

My wife and I have had the joy of being involved with planting and watering numerous churches through the years. When we went to Budapest to lead the planting there, our family stayed all together in one dorm room. We would go out every day with the small permanent team and the small temporary team to evangelize. (We were temporary on this planting.) We handed out thousands of invitations, about 160 came to the first service, and some started studying the Bible right away. A few became Christians quickly.

As we go out in faith, not everything goes the way it gets planned. In flying over to help with the Bucharest, Romania planting, our son became quite ill. It became apparent while catching our connecting flight in Paris that he needed to go to the hospital for some emergency surgery due to an acute appendicitis. It was so critical that if we had traveled on, he could have died. A few days after the operation, my daughter and I continued on to Bucharest to share our faith and to be there for the first service. It had been prearranged for many of the German brothers and sisters to come and evangelize for this first service and so there was an army of faith there to help. In the end, God worked everything out as 516 people came to the first service and many started to study the Bible right away. Very soon, there were some who were baptized into Christ.

For a decade, my wife and I had the honor and privilege to plan and oversee a European Missions Conference. This conference started small, but every year it grew larger to the point of having thousands in attendance. One year it was held in Berlin, but in the other years it took place in Paris, France. On one of those occasions, the theme for the conference was ALL NATIONS. Disciples from throughout Europe met to sing and preach and fellowship and dance and baptize in the beautiful Palais des Congrès. At that time I wrote lyrics for a song to highlight the theme. As you read these words, have faith that you can help others come eye to eye with God, and that all nations can be changed for the glory of God!

**ALL NATIONS**

Randy McKean (Updated Version)

I went to the wall
Where East and West call
To join in a world-shaking ball.
Skinheads and armies,
Neo-Nazis and all
Maintaining and building a wall.
Where was the fall?
Where was the fall
Of this deadly wall?
Where was the fall?
Where was the fall
Of this deadly wall?
Something broke out inside of me.
As more and more people came out to see,
All I heard them say to me
Is...Can you set me free?

*All Nations—*
*Gotta go eye to eye.*
*All Nations—*
*Gotta go eye to eye.*

The sunrise appears;
The world is in fear;
No food and no clothes and so many tears.
Starving children aborted and trashed,
Abused by the arms
That draw them near.
Where are the ears?

Where are the ears
Of the people who hear?
Where are the ears?
Where are the ears
Of the people who hear?
Something broke out inside of me.
As more and more people came out to see,
All I heard them say to me
Is...Can you set me free?

*All Nations—Gotta go eye to eye.*
*All Nations—Gotta go eye to eye.*

New York is a place
Where many a face
Shows the tragedy of the waste.
Times Square and Sinatra set up the pace;
Bin Laden and bombers
Take their place.
Where was the case?
Where was the case
Of this terrorist's face?
Where was the case?
Where was the case
Of this terrorist's face?
Something broke out inside of me.
As more and more people came out to see,
All I heard them say to me
Is...Can you set me free?

*All Nations—Gotta go eye to eye.*
*All Nations—Gotta go eye to eye.*

*See all nations going eye to eye—See all nations going eye to eye.*
*See all nations going eye to eye—See all nations going eye to eye.*
*See all nations going eye to eye—See all nations going eye to eye.*

# FAITH SECRET 9

## Financial Faith

The ninth faith secret is contained in the subject of Financial Faith—actually a few secrets are here for us! The Bible has much to say about money. Its instructions include: stay out of debt, use money to help others, give to the poor, don't love it and gather it little by little to make it grow. We are to pursue wisdom and not money, and no one can serve both God and money. We should put our money to work and estimate costs before buying anything. In the Bible, we are shown examples of those who sold their property and used the money to support ministry. We're commanded not to be greedy, but to enjoy what money can buy, to use money for good deeds and to be generous. We are taught to be free from the love of money and to be content with what we have. Believe it or not, all this teaching fits perfectly together. None of it is contradictory when we look at the Scriptures with a balanced interpretation and correct application.

The Bible provides extensive instruction regarding money because how we view and use money affects our faith and demonstrates our faithfulness to God. The main question is not: "How much (or how little) do you have in the bank?" The main question is: "How much (or how little) do you trust in God regardless of how much or how little you have in the bank?" Where do we really put our security in life? Greed tempts the rich and the poor. Those with modest means may fall into discontent, falsely believing that if they only possessed more money, they would be more faithful. The rich succumb to greed when, like the people of Sodom, they become *"arrogant, overfed and unconcerned; they did not help the poor and needy."*

While this chapter provides some practical instruction, the intent is to illustrate the relationship between money and faith by defining three financial faith principles combined with three associated faith secrets.

## PRINCIPLE 1: What You Give Is What You Get
## SECRET: *God will give you even more!*

> *"Give, and it will be given to you. A good measure, pressed down, shaken together and running over, will be poured into your lap. For with the measure you use, it will be measured to you." (Luke 6:38)*

I don't believe this verse is strictly talking about money, but it certainly includes the subject of money. This is a universal truth that God has built into the human condition. When you give, you will get back according to what you have given. Jesus taught that there is a direct correlation between giving and getting back.

**Give a Little → Get Back a Little**
**Give Nothing → Get Back Nothing**
**Give Much → Get Back Much**

When I give a little love, I will get back a little love. When I give a little encouragement, I will get back a little encouragement. When I give much forgiveness, I will receive back much forgiveness. When I give much compassion, I will receive back much compassion. When I give much anger, I will receive back much anger. When I give nothing, I will get back nothing in return. You could say it's a live-by-the-sword, die-by-the-sword kind of thing (Matthew 26:52). So when it comes to money, according to Jesus, I receive as I give. It may or may not return in cold hard cash, but it will be in something valuable and desirable.

Here is the faith secret attached to this financial principle: *God will give you even more!* When it comes to God, he goes way beyond the measurement we use. He makes sure that his measurement is, first of all, pressed down. He wants to make sure as much fits in as possible. Then he shakes it. That's to ensure there are no air pockets or empty spaces hidden in the measurement. But then he overfills it to the point that it runs into our laps! It's like going to Five Guys for a hamburger and fries. Besides having the best burgers around, the way they serve their fries is awesome. When they measure them, they first of all fill up whatever size container you ordered, then they shake it to put some more in and then they place your order in a bag. But finally they throw on top of your fries another big portion of fries. The container is now overflowing with them! We all like getting more than we deserve, and that's what God does with us: we all get more than we deserve. Not just a little more, a lot more. An abundance. Even those who give him nothing receive from God good things to enjoy in this life. God is such a generous God. So, with the measure you use, it will be measured to you. But with God, he will give you even more!

## PRINCIPLE 2: Your Priorities Follow Your Treasure SECRET: *God will give you peace!*

> *"Do not store up for yourselves treasures on earth… But store up for yourselves treasures in heaven… For where your treasure is your heart will be also… You cannot serve both God and money…*
>
> *"Do not worry about your life…*
>
> *"Will he not much more clothe you — you of little faith?... For the pagans run after all these things, and your heavenly Father knows that you need them. But seek first his kingdom and his righteousness, and all these things will be given to you as well." (Matthew 6:19–33)*

Jesus tells us that our priorities follow our treasure. In fact, what we treasure affects our trust or faith in God. If our heart's desire is accumulating money and possessions, that's a treasure problem that leads to a priority problem. He never said that accumulating money and things was in itself a problem. The root of the issue has to do with our treasure. The passage above makes it clear that our heart follows our treasure. And where are hearts are, our priorities will be. Therefore, we must have the right treasure to have the right priorities. Our treasure must be in what is eternal. Let's remember that we can't take it with us. Rockefeller accumulated a net worth of 392 billion dollars (in today's dollars that would be 663 billion). How much did he leave? He left all of it! There is never a U-Haul following a hearse. The first priority in a person's heart must be love for God. God himself is to be our greatest treasure. We will always love the most what we treasure the most. The result will be God's priorities become our priorities. We find from this passage of Scripture that of first importance to God are his kingdom and his righteousness. So as his children, what God loves, we are to love. What God says is most important must be most important to us. Although challenging at times, having and maintaining the correct priorities is from the God ordained outcome of storing up heavenly treasure instead of storing up earthly treasure. And, it will be obvious to everyone what you treasure the most. Your priorities say it all because your priorities *always* follow your treasure.

To seek "*first*" means to seek God's will primarily in everything you do and decide. "First" here is not the word for order placement. You don't just get up and the very first thing you do is something for God and then you're done for the day. The word for "*first*" here indicates that seeking first his kingdom and his righteousness invades every area and every hour of our lives in every action and in every choice that is made.

Jesus says to seek first God's kingdom. God's kingdom on earth includes everyone who makes him king; all who are citizens of heaven; his holy bride, the church. In one of Jesus' parables (Matthew 13:44), he taught that the kingdom is like a treasure hidden in a field and when a person finds that treasure it is worth selling everything to have it. A person does this because they are convinced the treasure (the kingdom) is more precious and more valuable than anything they presently possess or will ever possess. God's kingdom must always remain our treasure. Considering this from a personal perspective, I must determine that my life decisions, including my financial life decisions, are no longer based on what is best for me or what I want to do. Rather, I must make my decisions on the basis of what is best for others in God's kingdom and what will help God's kingdom grow and thrive the most. A person does this happily and willingly if the kingdom is their treasure.

As we seek first God's kingdom, we also seek first his righteousness. We do what will advance a right relationship with God. Again let it be said that our greatest treasure is God himself. Having and maintaining a right relationship with God is to be the most precious aspect of our lives. Therefore, with every decision a person is to ask themselves, "What is the *right* or *righteous* thing to do?" And let's remember that for the moment we are concentrating on what is the right *financial* thing to do. Whether in a business decision, a personal decision, a family decision, a marriage decision, a small decision or a big decision, you are to seek the answer to what would please God the most in your relationship with him. It is important to point out that so many decisions in life do have a financial component to them.

There is a faith secret attached to this financial principle as well: *God will give you peace!* Isn't that amazing? When I treasure and prioritize correctly and put into practice all of God's wisdom about finances, I no longer have to worry and run after what the pagans (faithless people) run after. When a priority problem turns into a worry problem, it can cause stress. With stress comes all kinds of health issues, such as high blood pressure, stroke or heart attack. So, the benefit of the peace God gives in financial faith will even allow you to live longer as you live better, knowing that God promises that your needs will be met. That's great news! You can be at peace just by doing what he says to do financially, morally and primarily in life. Remember, though, that since life is always changing, you have to continually protect your priorities. As you journey through the different seasons of life, you must keep God's kingdom and God's righteousness as your treasure. By protecting your priority, you protect your faith. When your treasure is in heavenly things, you hold to your priorities and God will give you peace!

## PRINCIPLE 3: Tithing—NO! Generosity—YES!<br>SECRET: *God will make you rich!*

Please read the following scriptures slowly and carefully. Take in each word and the meaning of each sentence anew. For the Christian, we are to delight in our standard of giving, not our standard of living.

> *"Will a mere mortal rob God? Yet you rob me.*
>
> *"But you ask, 'How are we robbing you?'*
>
> *"In tithes and offerings. You are under a curse — your whole nation — because you are robbing me. Bring the whole tithe into the storehouse, that there may be food in my house. Test me in this," says the LORD Almighty, "and see if I will not throw open the floodgates of heaven and pour out so much blessing that there will not be room enough to store it. I will prevent pests from devouring your crops, and the vines in your fields will not drop their fruit before it is ripe," says the LORD Almighty. "Then all the nations will call you blessed, for yours will be a delightful land," says the LORD Almighty. (Malachi 3:8–12)*

> *Remember this: Whoever sows sparingly will also reap sparingly, and whoever sows generously will also reap generously. Each of you should give what you have decided in your heart to give, not reluctantly or under compulsion, for God loves a cheerful giver. And God is able to bless you abundantly, so that in all things at all times, having all that you need, you will abound in every good work. As it is written:*
>
> *"They have freely scattered their gifts to the poor;*
> *their righteousness endures forever."*

*Now he who supplies seed to the sower and bread for food will also supply and increase your store of seed and will enlarge the harvest of your righteousness. You will be enriched in every way so that you can be generous on every occasion. (2 Corinthians 9:6–11a)*

*For you know the grace of our Lord Jesus Christ, that though he was rich, yet for your sake he became poor, so that you through his poverty might become rich. (2 Corinthians 8:9)*

What is God saying and not saying with these scriptures? This section is not an exhaustive study of the practice of giving, but let's do some background work so that we come to the right faith conclusions. The word "tithe" means "one tenth." The Israelites gave a proportion of their income as offerings to express thankfulness, honor and dedication to God. In the agrarian society of the Old Testament, tithes were not paid in cash, gold or goods but in crops or livestock. (If you lived a long distance away from the place of offering, you could sell your first fruits, bring money, and then buy what was needed for feasts or sacrifices.) The Israelites gave a one-tenth offering of their increase representing the best and the first fruits of their harvest. From Old Testament passages, it appears there were actually three tithes in the Old Testament. Two tithes were offered every year and one tithe every three years, or an average of 23.3% of one's yearly produce from the land. There were also provisions for freewill offerings and personal giving beyond the tithes. Therefore, the tithe never stood alone. The three tithes were used in three main ways: to support full-time workers (the Levitical, or sacred tithe in Numbers 18:21, 24), to provide meals for community celebration and fellowship (the tithe of the feasts in Deuteronomy 14:22–27) and the tithe every three years to primarily help the poor and needy (Deuteronomy 26:12). It is interesting to note that the second tithe would translate today into being like the money we should budget each year to spend on conferences, retreats, preteen and teen camps, youth corps offerings, mission trips and other special fellowship and ministry opportunities.

Tithes were given by the patriarchs Abraham (Genesis 14:17–20) and Jacob (Genesis 28:22). Later a system of tithes was instituted in the Law of God given through Moses (Deuteronomy 12, 14, 26). The prophets, like Malachi, strongly corrected the Israelites for not giving their *"tithes and offerings"* to God. Notice these words are both in the plural form. As you look at this, you can easily realize that the tithe was never *the* standard of Old Testament generosity. It went beyond it. Nor is it *the* standard for Christian generosity. And I can't imagine any first-century Jewish convert deciding to give less to the work of God because of the decision to become a Christian. Still, tithing is a helpful guideline as we strive to develop a lifestyle of generosity.

So what are Christians called to? The tithe, or tenth, is mentioned in four chapters (Matthew 23; Luke 11; Luke 18; Hebrews 7) in the New Testament, but none of these are used as a command for Christians to tithe. At the same time, nothing is said in these passages that would command a Christian *not* to tithe. In fact, Christians are called to even greater and more extravagant freewill giving in response to the sacrifice Jesus has given to us. Our giving is based on faith in God as our provider. So instead of settling for giving ten percent, we should note the command to give generously, just as Jesus gave to us. It is interesting to see that John the Baptizer raised the standard to fifty percent giving in one situation (Luke 3:11) and Jesus was pleased with 100 percent giving from the poor widow (Luke 21:1–4). There will be times and situations when individuals happily give half of something or even all of it to God! For example we give 50 to 100 percent of our tax return money each year to our Special Missions Contribution. I know of others who have given to God a large portion of their bonus money or of their inheritance money. So, the fact that the tithe is not mentioned for Christians is not evidence that God expects less, but that far more is possible. The tithe is still a helpful guideline, since it reminds us to give proportionally to God as he blesses us. We are to honor him with a portion even as we understand that he owns it all. Although the tithe no longer applies in the same way for Christians, God's reasons for giving—ministers, mission, worship, fellowship and the poor—have not changed.

As Christians living under the New Covenant, we have so much more than those who were living under the Old Covenant. We have Jesus as our redeemer. We have the Spirit of God living inside of us. We have been shown more revealed truth and more revealed mysteries than ever before. And so with all of this in view, to just apply tithe laws would be trite and shallow. Tithing for the Christian should be viewed as a good starting point for a lifetime of ever-growing Christian giving. The standard in the New Testament is much more radical than simple tithing. We are told to give what we have decided in our hearts to give, not reluctantly or under compulsion, and to do so cheerfully. Our freedom in Christ is to cultivate voluntary generosity. Our freedom in Christ means there is no minimum and there is no maximum to our giving. It is freedom to excel in the grace of giving. It is freedom to give more, not less. So how much do we give? The word that is used most in the Bible to describe Christian giving is the word "generous." We are to give generously as we are guided and inspired by Jesus' sacrificial example: *"that though he was rich, yet for your sake he became poor, so that you through his poverty might become rich."* We also give generously because we are guided and inspired by the example of other Christians like the ones from Macedonia who set the bar high by giving out of their extreme poverty. Certainly there will be a difference in the total amount contributed from First World giving compared to Third World giving but the word "generous" is to describe all Christian giving regardless of one's personal circumstance. In the end, it's not the amount you give; it's the amount of generosity it represents for you when you give that reveals a person's faith.

**Little Generosity reveals Little Faith**
**No Generosity reveals No Faith**
**Much Generosity reveals Much Faith**

What is the faith secret attached to this financial principle? *God will make you rich!* By saying this here, I may have lost some of you for a moment. No, the Bible does not teach the "prosperity gospel," in which the motivation to give financially is to become rich financially. Although it's true that financial gains are a blessing from God, it's not true that God's blessings are always financial. The Bible says that *"you will be enriched* (made rich) *in every way so that you can be generous on every occasion."* The Bible also says to test God and see if he will not *"throw open the floodgates of heaven and pour out so much blessing that there will not be room enough to store it."* He makes us rich, but not necessarily with money and possessions. He makes us rich in the things that are most important in life, such as a sense of belonging, being loved, having meaningful family relationships, experiencing genuine care and concern from others and receiving help in times of need. God's purpose of giving us wealth (of all kinds) is so we can share with others. God gives us enough material wealth for us to be generous on all occasions. So God promises that our giving is always to our benefit. But in our practice of giving we should never give just for the economic benefits it might bring. Thinking back to the discussion on seeking first his righteousness, being generous is a main way our righteousness endures forever (2 Corinthians 9:9). Our goals in giving will be to honor God, to be grateful and to glorify God. In doing this, we reveal the depth and amount of faith we have in God providing all we need. So to tithing say, "NO!" to generosity say, "YES!" and God will make you rich!

## Two Stories

Although there are many stories I could tell you, I will limit myself to sharing just two about the financial workings of God in my life. This first story illustrates how God gives to us more than we deserve (overflowing in our laps). It also shows how we need to say "no" to money opportunities if the situation is not spiritually safe or best. And finally, the story illustrates how we can use God's blessings to teach our children the proper heart in giving back to God. When my son was fourteen and my daughter seventeen, I heard an advertisement on the radio about modeling. I thought that it would be something fun to try and would also provide a way to meet people that we could invite to church. We discussed the possibilities as a family, and after getting some advice from others, we participated in a weekend modeling conference. During that weekend we reached out to people, which led to ten people coming to church with us that Sunday! At the end of the conference my daughter was interviewed by LA Models. They wanted her to move to LA and start her career. Although thrilled she was chosen, that wasn't what we had in mind since moving would not be a wise spiritual decision; she was still a junior in high school! My son was chosen to work for both a New York firm and a Boston firm. Since we lived in Boston at that time, we were able to work with that. A few months later, Kent landed a national television commercial that had him riding on an Oreo cookie for Nabisco. We really had no idea how all of this worked, but he started to get checks in the mail. To make a long story short, our eighth grade son made $100,000 that year! His success didn't continue like that, but it was fun while it lasted. As the checks came in, we would sit down and talk about it all being a blessing from God and that he should honor God by giving a tithe. He was excited about being able to give to God, and that is what he faithfully did with every penny he earned. In time, the income from his modeling job helped Kent pay for a portion of his college tuition, an engagement ring, a honeymoon and a house.

Another time in life illustrates both my failure to financially plan well and God pouring out his blessings. This is when my daughter was close to her senior year of high school and everything seemed to focus on colleges. I was trying to figure out how in the world we could possibly pay for it. We had previously sold almost everything we owned to go on the mission field. We were happily giving generously to the church and to mission work. We had only a couple of thousand dollars in the bank. We were renting a home, paying on cars and barely keeping up with the bills as they came. With the thought about college tuition frequently on my mind, I made a trip to visit my parents. My dad loved to play golf, so I joined him out on the course. On one of the greens, just as I was about to putt the ball into the hole, my dad asked me, "Now, have I mentioned to you about the trust fund that your grandparents set up for the education of your kids?" No, he hadn't mentioned it and no, I knew nothing about it! But that trust fund meant that the kids could attend a good college without the worry of debt. Although it didn't cover everything, it certainly covered a lot! All I could do was to thank my God and my grandparents and my parents who added to the fund as time went along. Again, I saw God taking care of us. By faith, God gave us even more than what was imagined. And just so you know, after hearing about the trust fund, I didn't care how badly I was shooting on the golf course!

You may not have exactly the same financial blessings that we had, but I'm sure you can tell stories of how God has taken care of you. The principles of financial faith are true, although the circumstances will vary. As a reminder, here are the Financial Faith Principles and Secrets:

**PRINCIPLE 1: What You Give Is What You Get**
**SECRET:** ***God will give you even more!***

**PRINCIPLE 2: Your Priorities Follow Your Treasure**
**SECRET:** ***God will give you peace!***

## PRINCIPLE 3: Tithing—NO! Generosity—YES!
## SECRET: *God will make you rich!*

# FAITH SECRET 10

## Increasing Faith

We now come to the last of the 10 Faith Secrets. You will see that this faith secret is built on the ones that we have already discussed. How can a person increase their faith? For many, the answer to this question is quite difficult to grasp, as it seems so ethereal and mysterious. But the Bible, the word of God, reveals mysteries! It reveals to us what we as humans otherwise would not know. The fact is that increasing our faith is a logical process. We will now come to understand how it works. Too often people substitute humanistic thinking and effort for faith in God. Let's go to God's word and allow it to reveal the process of increasing faith.

> *Jesus said to his disciples: "Things that cause people to stumble are bound to come, but woe to anyone through whom they come. It would be better for them to be thrown into the sea with a millstone tied around their neck than to cause one of these little ones to stumble. So watch yourselves.*
>
> *"If your brother or sister sins against you, rebuke them; and if they repent, forgive them. Even if they sin against you seven times in a day and seven times come back to you saying 'I repent,' you must forgive them."*
>
> *The apostles said to the Lord,* ***"Increase our faith!"***
>
> *He replied, "If you have faith as small as a mustard seed, you can say to this mulberry tree, 'Be uprooted and planted in the sea,' and it will obey you.*
>
> *"Suppose one of you has a servant plowing or looking after the sheep. Will he say to the servant when he comes in from the field, 'Come along now and sit down to eat'? Won't he rather say, 'Prepare my supper, get yourself ready and wait on me while I eat and drink; after that you may eat and drink'? Will he thank the servant because he did what he was told to do? So you also, when you have done everything you were told to do, should say, 'We are unworthy servants; we have only done our duty.'" (Luke 17:1–10, emphasis added)*

Most people make the mistake of separating this into a few disconnected thoughts instead of realizing it is all one thoughtful conversation. People go to this passage to say we need to forgive a lot (and we do) or to find out how to be a great servant (which we also need to do). But we must read it in its context! The servant story was a portion of the answer that Jesus gave on how to increase faith. So let's now look at it more carefully.

In this conversation with the disciples, Jesus remarked that sin is inevitable; it is all around us. In other words, sin happens. But then he said quite strongly that there are serious consequences for those who cause someone to sin and stumble. And what a mental picture he gave here. Better for a person to have a millstone (a huge and heavy stone) tied around his neck and be thrown into the sea than to cause someone to stumble. I would say that's a pretty serious and "heavy" consequence!

Jesus then moved into a related subject about forgiveness when someone sins against you. How is that connected? By the fact that a person's failure to forgive can often lead others into sin. If a person is unforgiving and so becomes bitter and resentful, that bitterness and resentment can easily spill out of their mouth and into another's heart. So Jesus told the apostles to forgive a person when he repents. At this point they were fine with this teaching. They believed (they had enough faith) that they could live that one out. Then Jesus went on to say that they were to forgive a person even if they sinned against them seven times in the same day. At this point the apostles were resistant. They were totally with Jesus and loving what he was saying until he got to the seven-times-in-the-same-day part. They couldn't see themselves forgiving to that extent. It seemed more than just difficult. It seemed impossible! And they all said to Jesus: "*Increase our faith!*" Although the apostles wanted to believe and embrace this and knew it was a good and right teaching, they realized they did not have the faith to actually live it. So they asked Jesus to increase their faith. Everything he says after that is the answer to how to increase faith.

Now, the point here is not just increasing faith to obey the one, specific teaching that is being dealt with in the passage. It's a truth to learn for *anything* that we find extremely difficult or seemingly impossible for us to obey. This is for *anytime* we say "I can't" or "I just don't have the faith to do it." Notice the word that Jesus chose when he spoke of the mulberry tree doing something that seems impossible. Jesus said it will OBEY. He was starting to open the apostles' minds to the way of increasing their faith that would lead them to becoming obedient. In this specific case, to forgive a person seven times in a day. There can be movement (increased faith) that results from an uprooting and a planting. Disobedience and unbelief can be uprooted. Obedience and belief can be planted. Remember, we are all empowered to do whatever God has promised we can do or has commanded us to do. So whatever needs to be moved will OBEY you because of your faith in God.

So how does a person start? You start with whatever amount of faith you have. And according to Jesus, it doesn't matter how small a person's faith is. It can be the mustard seed kind of faith and, by the way, a mustard seed is literally quite tiny! The issue is not the starting point of a person's faith; the issue is that there is a starting point. (Note: If a person is unwilling to start to work on bringing themselves into obedience, then it's not a problem of faith in God; it's a problem of rebellion against God. Whenever a person says "No" to God, he is in rebellion against him.) The man we studied about earlier who cried, *"I believe; help me overcome my unbelief!"* is a great example of a person with little faith but who had the willingness to start working on his lack of faith.

So, you take the faith you have and you *start.* Question: Would you rather have small faith in a strong bridge or big faith in a weak bridge? The real issue is the condition of the bridge, not the amount of faith in crossing it. And so with us, the main thing is not the amount of our faith but what our faith is in. And since our faith is in God, we can start with small faith because it's faith in a strong and powerful God. Therefore, we can overcome what at first seems impossible for us to do, to accomplish, to become or to change. We first need to start with whatever amount of faith we have.

But how do we start? Jesus now tells us the story of the hardworking servant. But remember, this is still the answer to the apostles when they asked Jesus to *increase their faith*. We learn that a person increases faith by being a hardworking servant of God. Jesus sets up the following process:

1. Start with whatever small faith in God you have. (Always work from your own faith, not from someone else's, although we are to be inspired by other people's faith.)
2. With your small faith, set a small-faith goal. (Remember to visualize it—a God kind of faith!)
3. Be willing to do the hard work to attain the small-faith goal. (This includes much prayer!)
4. When the goal is attained, then your faith has been actualized. (Remember to thank God and to give him the glory!)
5. The result is a little increase in your faith seeing God at work as the small goal is realized.

Next a person takes that little-increased-faith and begins the process again.

1. Start with the little-increased faith in God you now have.
2. With your little-increased faith, set a little-increased-faith goal. (Still visualize it—a God kind of faith!)
3. Be willing to do the hard work to attain the little-increased-faith goal. (This includes much prayer!)
4. When the goal is attained, then your faith has been actualized. (Remember to thank God and to give him the glory!)

5. The result is a further increase in your faith seeing God at work as the little-increased goal is realized.

Again a person takes their further-increased-faith and begins the process again.

1. Start with the further-increased faith in God you now have.
2. With your further-increased faith, you can set a further-increased-faith goal. (Always visualize it! Have a God kind of faith!)
3. Be willing to do the hard work to attain the further-increased-faith goal. (This still includes much prayer!)
4. When the goal is attained, then your faith has been actualized. (Continue to remember to thank God and to give him the glory!)
5. The result is a continued increase in your faith seeing God at work as the further-increased goal is realized.

This process of increasing one's faith is unending. A man or woman of faith will always have some kind of faith goal for some area of their lives and will always be exerting the needed work to attain the goal. Then each time a person sees their faith goal become a reality, or actualized, there will be an increase of personal faith in God. This process continues until a person has much faith concerning the area they have been concentrating on. This is what people mean when they say "step out in faith." It means to try something you know you can't do on your own. It means striving to obey God in something where you have to rely on him for help. It's moving out of your comfort zone. It's knowing that for you, on your own power, it seems quite difficult if not impossible to do or to obey. But now you understand the God-ordained process behind it. Now you know that God's plan is to start you with your faith wherever it is at. God then moves you forward in your faith with steps or increments of faith that will lead to having an increased faith.

The hard work that is to be done is the work that God specifies us to do. Then the work we are doing is "*work produced by faith*" (1 Thessalonians 1:3a) and not some humanistic work to achieve a goal. Remember our earlier discussion of mission faith. God has specific work we are to do to be fruitful: scattering the seed, which is the word of God; finding a worthy person to teach, etc. By doing the work exactly the way God tells us to do it, the work is not a humanistic thing, it's a faith thing. It's the way God made both the spiritual and the physical universe to behave. And specified hard work is just a part of the process. We are simply doing and believing in what God says to do.

But there is more to learn here about increasing faith. The servant is *consistently* out in the field or taking care of the sheep. A servant works every day. So the fact that it is daily is a big part of the hard work. As he is serving, we see that *self comes last* as he does much work for the master before he meets his own needs. With this, he does not accuse the master of being selfish. He knows that his reason for existence is to be a bondservant of the master, who in the story represents God. A hired servant has some rights, but a bondservant (slave) has no rights. The bondservant totally belongs to the master. And this is the kind of servant being discussed in this passage of Scripture.

Then we see that this servant follows through by doing all the specifics of the work that he was given to accomplish. The passage states it in these words: he did *everything he had been told to do.* And in the end, he has a very humble attitude. He wasn't looking for a pat on the back or a prize for all that he had accomplished. His attitude is demonstrated in the last description from Jesus about the servant being an unworthy servant who was just doing his duty. He did a lot of great work, but he did not think himself great. If he had given credit and glory to himself, he would have demonstrated that his faith was in himself or that his faith in God was for himself. If this had been done, faith would have still increased, but it would have been faith in self increasing, instead of faith in God increasing. When we truly believe our works are accomplished through the extraordinary power of God, it is easy to give God the glory.

Here are some examples of situations in which a person may need to increase faith to become obedient to God.

- **Example 1:** Overcoming a particular sin may seem difficult to impossible. I have known many people dealing with drugs (including nicotine), alcohol or pornography. They felt like it was impossible to change. The longevity, the shame, and the defeat were very deep in their lives. But as they took the small faith they had and started to go to work on their issue *exactly the way God said to do it*, they started to see victories. This would certainly include such things as bringing everything into the light through confession of sin, developing relationships that give loving accountability, having daily encouragement through daily relationships, and being radical about removing temptations and accessibility. From those victories, they took their increased faith and made increasing expectations for themselves. They continued to have success, and that built more and more faith. They eventually moved to the point of total obedience and so they now have *much faith or increased faith* about being able to overcome their sin. And they give God the credit for the success, not themselves. They know that without a continued close walk with God, they could go back to their old ways. They must remain reliant on God.

- **Example 2:** I have done marriage counseling with a number of couples who have fallen out of love. They lost the feelings they formerly had for each other and felt lonely, unhappy and unfulfilled. They had to be willing to start the daily hard work (to be hard-working bondservants) and start doing the loving actions and saying the loving words regardless of the lack of feelings. You don't wait for the right feelings before doing the right actions! The Bible demonstrates that if we do the right actions, the right feelings will follow, although of course there are always the hurts and disappointments that have to be talked out, and also expectations and needs must be discussed. But I have seen it again and again: couples taking their small faith and starting to work on their marriages. Eventually, God has led them back to having a strong, loving marriage. At that point, they have much faith that their marriage can be happy and fulfilling as they have taken control of their feelings and moved them by making their feelings OBEY them. (They moved the mulberry tree!) And they give God the credit for the change. They shout gladly, "Look how God saved our marriage!"

- **Example 3:** Forgiving a person or persons after experiencing deep hurt and pain may seem difficult to impossible. I think we have all been there at different points in our lives. I know I have. At times in my life I knew I was to forgive, and so I would do some of the right things like pray for individuals and make myself remember the good times together. On some occasions, I even talked myself into thinking I had forgiven from the heart. What I found out from later face-to-face conversations was that I hadn't really forgiven. I still wanted them to understand how much pain and hurt they had put me through. Or I still wanted to hear someone say they were wrong in their actions or say how sorry they were. As I have tried at different times with different people to work through the issues in my heart, I knew I would need to get to the point of total obedience. The Bible says to *"forgive as the Lord forgave you"* (Colossians 3:13b). After years of being a Christian, I came to understand that no one will really understand the degree of pain another person goes through. I came to understand that there may never be agreement on specific actions taken or not taken. And there may never be the exact words spoken you think you need to hear. At different times, I have had to accept and reaccept those facts at my emotional core. To do that, I had to see clearly where I had failed, what I could have done better and how I had reacted in unrighteous ways. The ultimate humbling came not from just knowing the right words and the right concepts about forgiveness from the Bible. I had to get down to all the gunk in my heart and remember in a deep way all my sin through all my life against God. And then I had to remember that God has forgiven me of all of it! I will never understand the degree of pain I have put God through because of my sin. My words have been inadequate to express my sorrow about my sin against God. And I know there are times I have not even been aware of my sin. But he is willing to forgive me. It may sound a little bizarre but, at times, I have had to work hard to remember the enormous amount of forgiveness and mercy I personally need and have graciously been given by God. Knowing he does not count my sin against me moves me to not count someone else's sin against them!

I had to take the small faith I had about a situation and start doing the right things with it. I kept that up (sometimes for years) until I finally got to the right place before God. Throughout my life, my faith has become stronger about being able to forgive others who have hurt or damaged or taken advantage of me in some way. In the process, I have become a more merciful person. In the end, we are all damaged people. We are damaged by our own sins and by the sins of others. The question is not whether or not we are damaged, but whether we are allowing ourselves to be controlled by the damage. At different periods in my life, I had to ask myself if I was going to allow the hurts, pains and disappointments in life to control me or if I was going to allow God to control me. There's always some hard work to do to get to the point of obedience. And, to be totally honest, there can be some triggers that bring up weird feelings about an old situation again. I just have to tell myself that I have already fully forgiven. It forces me to remember how much God has forgiven me. So, faith can be increased to the point that we can successfully obey *any* of God's commandments including, *"Forgive as the Lord forgave you."*

If you want to increase your faith, you must positively embrace being a hard-working bondservant (slave) of God. You must gladly desire to please God (your master) in every way. We can never act like we have any rights of our own, because we were bought at a price—redeemed by the death of Jesus. You must plan to do what you know is very difficult, if not impossible, to accomplish by your own power. You must desire to bring yourself into obedience to the commands of God. Then you must consistently (daily) work by doing all that God directs you to do. You must do it with all your might and focus, knowing God will supply what you lack and believing that he will ultimately make your faith goals a reality. As the changes or the opportunities or the abilities come, you must remember to give the thanks and the glory to God. He has done it, not you. You are to start from wherever your faith is at, even if it's a mustard-seed-sized faith...but you START!

This closes out the Faith Secrets with Faith Secret 10...

**how to have Increasing Faith.**

# PART FOUR

# JOYFUL FAITH

You have just learned 10 FAITH SECRETS. Now it's time to embrace the right attitude of faith as we go through our lives. This attitude of faith makes all the difference. The kind of faith that God desires us to have is a joyful faith. God wants us to be overcomers—to overcome discouragement, fatigue and failure. God wants us to live a victorious life. The apostle Paul certainly went through some very challenging times in his life, but he had and maintained a joyful faith relying on God.

> *We do not want you to be uninformed, brothers and sisters, about the troubles we experienced in the province of Asia. We were under great pressure, far beyond our ability to endure, so that we despaired of life itself. Indeed, we felt we had received the sentence of death. But this happened that we might not rely on ourselves but on God, who raises the dead. (2 Corinthians 1:8–9)*

Everybody gets discouraged. Everybody gets tired. Everybody fails at one time or another. We are all tempted to quit, give in or settle for mediocrity. We have health problems or child-raising challenges. At times, Christians disappoint us—they let us down. Sometimes they even sin against us! We have to deal with fruitlessness, marriage challenges and financial pressures. There can be setbacks in our work, our schooling or our church. There are times when we are taken advantage of and there may be besetting sins in our lives. On top of this there is the exhaustion from taking care of the children and the monotony of housework or the job. We can be mistreated, misrepresented and misunderstood. The list of troubles could go on and on.

Then there are the feelings the troubles of life can produce in us as we go through them. We can start thinking: "No one really cares"... "I'm not important"... "I can't do anything right." Questions could start lingering in our minds like "Is this Christianity stuff real?" or "Is it worth all this?" There could be thoughts like "I'm no good to anyone" or "I can't do it" or "What's the use in even trying?" It's times like these that can lead a person into becoming critical, numb, uncaring or cynical.

But God wants us to live with a joyful faith as we go through all the ups and downs in life. In this section, we will be looking at Paul's joyful faith. As we do, we will be asking the question, what made Paul tick? What was going on in Paul's head that made him able to overcome discouragement, fatigue and failure so that he could consistently live a victorious Christian life?

*Whatever you have learned or received or heard from me, or seen in me — put it into practice. And the God of peace will be with you. (Philippians 4:9)*

Paul says, What you see in me...DO! If you imitate this man's faith in your life, then you will reproduce this man's results in your life. Let's now look into his life. When Paul preached, he dispelled apathy. People either responded warmly or they opposed it violently.

*In Lystra there sat a man who was lame. He had been that way from birth and had never walked. He listened to Paul as he was speaking. Paul looked directly at him, saw that he had faith to be healed and called out, "Stand up on your feet!" At that, the man jumped up and began to walk.*

*When the crowd saw what Paul had done, they shouted in the Lycaonian language, "The gods have come down to us in human form!" Barnabas they called Zeus, and Paul they called Hermes because he was the chief speaker. The priest of Zeus, whose temple was just outside the city, brought bulls and wreaths to the city gates because he and the crowd wanted to offer sacrifices to them.*

*But when the apostles Barnabas and Paul heard of this, they tore their clothes and rushed out into the crowd, shouting: "Friends, why are you doing this? We too are only*

> *human, like you. We are bringing you good news, telling you to turn from these worthless things to the living God, who made the heavens and the earth and the sea and everything in them. In the past, he let all nations go their own way. Yet he has not left himself without testimony: He has shown kindness by giving you rain from heaven and crops in their seasons; he provides you with plenty of food and fills your hearts with joy." Even with these words, they had difficulty keeping the crowd from sacrificing to them.*
>
> *Then some Jews came from Antioch and Iconium and won the crowd over. They stoned Paul and dragged him outside the city, thinking he was dead. But after the disciples had gathered around him, he got up and went back into the city. The next day he and Barnabas left for Derbe. (Acts 14:8–20)*

They stoned Paul! Think about what that means. Paul was being hit with stones over and over again. He was beaten up halfway through his message and dragged out of the city. He was unconscious, bloody and bruised to such a degree that he was thought to be dead. Paul's followers were certainly ill at ease (to say the least) with their leader being stoned. Just imagine this scene: the followers are leaning over him, and all of a sudden Paul opens his eyes! He says, "What are you guys doing?" The followers say, "Well, we were just planning your funeral." And then Paul gets up and starts walking. The followers yell, "That's the wrong way, Paul! You're heading back into the city." They're thinking that he must be delirious. But Paul just smiles and says, "I'm going back...and you're coming too!"

That's joyful faith in action! So why go back? It's very simple, really. Paul hadn't finished his sermon. That takes guts, and you know what's needed today? Christians with guts! We can look at other groups with lesser aims and false causes, and they are willing to die for what they believe in. How much more do we need to be gutsy Christians? When you can look danger in the face and demonstrate courage, that is joyful faith! As an extra bonus, you'll feel great about yourself. When you do right, you feel right. Now remember what Paul said: *what you see in me...DO!*

Let's go to another time in Paul's life when he was sharing the good news of Jesus. Today, if a special speaker comes into town, you may ask the person if he or she has a preference of a hotel or with whom they would like to stay. When Paul visited a new city, he would check out the prison, because he knew he would be in it before the week was through! He would have a starting night or day and it would end when they locked him up. Kind of fun!

> *The next day Agrippa and Bernice came with great pomp and entered the audience room with the high-ranking military officers and the prominent men of the city. At the command of Festus, Paul was brought in. Festus said: "King Agrippa, and all who are present with us, you see this man! The whole Jewish community has petitioned me about him in Jerusalem and here in Caesarea, shouting that he ought not to live any longer. I found he had done nothing deserving of death, but because he made his appeal to the Emperor I decided to send him to Rome. But I have nothing definite to write to His Majesty about him. Therefore I have brought him before all of you, and especially before you, King Agrippa, so that as a result of this investigation I may have something to write. For I think it is unreasonable to send a prisoner on to Rome without specifying the charges against him." (Acts 25:23–27)*

Paul has been in prison for some time. As he is shoved from gloom and darkness into the bright light of day, Paul is trying his best to see clearly; it's like coming out of a dark movie theater into bright daylight. He starts to make out two forms—two thrones—a king and a queen. He sees distinguished people sitting all around. These are the nobility and the people who were working hard to become nobility. It also included those who, no matter how hard they worked, would never become nobility. All were there and all were looking down on Paul. Straight from his cell, Paul is a smelly, dirty mess, shackled by his chains.

"*Then Agrippa said to Paul, 'You have permission to speak for yourself*'" (Acts 26:1). Paul is told to speak. What would you have said? Maybe "I haven't prepared" or "I forgot my notes" or "I require a three-day notice." But look at Paul's reaction: "*King Agrippa, I consider myself fortunate to stand before you today as I make my defense against all the accusations of the Jews*" (Acts 6:2).

He basically says, "I'm very happy to be here...in fact thrilled and excited to be here!" It's fun to have Christianity like this. Everything is stacked against you, yet you know what it is to be delighted, to consider yourself fortunate. That's joyful faith! It's the ability to roll with the punches. It's the ability to move into a situation where everything is going wrong and come up with the right answers. Paul is at ease when talking with the king and queen. Soon, he was the only person at ease in the whole place. Paul preached. In fact, he even gave an invitation—a very specific invitation.

> *At this point Festus interrupted Paul's defense. "You are out of your mind, Paul!" he shouted. "Your great learning is driving you insane."*
>
> *"I am not insane, most excellent Festus," Paul replied. "What I am saying is true and reasonable. The king is familiar with these things, and I can speak freely to him. I am convinced that none of this has escaped his notice, because it was not done in a corner. King Agrippa, do you believe the prophets? I know you do."*
>
> *Then Agrippa said to Paul, "Do you think that in such a short time you can persuade me to be a Christian?"*
>
> *Paul replied, "Short time or long — I pray to God that not only you but all who are listening to me today may become what I am, except for these chains." (Acts 26:24–29)*

Paul was happily persuading men to be Christians. To demonstrate conviction in the face of doubt is joyful faith! When everyone else is unsure—you are sure. You know who you believe; you know what you believe. You know why you believe. Faith is being firm. Faith is being solid. Faith is being sure.

On another occasion, Paul was in prison.

> *The crowd joined in the attack against Paul and Silas, and the magistrates ordered them to be stripped and beaten with rods. After they had been severely flogged, they were thrown into prison, and the jailer was commanded to guard them carefully. When he received these orders, he put them in the inner cell and fastened their feet in the stocks.*
>
> *About midnight Paul and Silas were praying and singing hymns to God, and the other prisoners were listening to them. Suddenly there was such a violent earthquake that the foundations of the prison were shaken. At once all the prison doors flew open, and everyone's chains came loose. The jailer woke up, and when he saw the prison doors open, he drew his sword and was about to kill himself because he thought the prisoners had*

*escaped. But Paul shouted, "Don't harm yourself! We are all here!"*

*The jailer called for lights, rushed in and fell trembling before Paul and Silas. He then brought them out and asked, "Sirs, what must I do to be saved?" (Acts 16:22–30)*

Paul's and Silas' feet are in stocks. They are in the inner cell. Their backs are torn flesh so they can't lean on anything. So Paul says to Silas, "Are you asleep?" Silas groggily says, "I *finally* was." Now Paul says, "Well, since you are awake, do you know of any good songs?" "Can't think of one" says Silas. Then Paul replies, "No worries, I'll teach you one." So they start singing. Now, obviously the singing must have been very bad, because it brought on an earthquake! Paul organizes the prisoners so that no one leaves. Then we see the jailer who wanted to commit suicide commit himself to Christ instead! This was a tough situation, and yet Paul is singing and praying to God. What is going on inside him at this point? We find the answer in the book of James: *"Is anyone among you in trouble? Let them pray. Is anyone happy? Let them sing songs of praise"* (James 5:13).

Is Paul in trouble? Yes! So he prays. Is Paul happy? Yes! So he sings. That's joyful faith! And be sure to remember what Paul wrote to us in Philippians: *what you see in me...DO!*

Still we come to another incident in Paul's life. He is now onboard a ship on his way to Rome where he will be on trial before Caesar.

*Much time had been lost, and sailing had already become dangerous because by now it was after the Day of Atonement. So Paul warned them, "Men, I can see that our voyage is going to be disastrous and bring great loss to ship and cargo, and to our own lives also." But the centurion, instead of listening to what Paul said, followed the advice of the pilot and of the owner of the ship. Since the harbor was unsuitable to winter in, the majority decided that we should sail on, hoping to reach Phoenix and winter there. This was a harbor in Crete, facing both southwest and northwest. (Acts 27:9–12)*

Certainly the centurion (a Roman soldier in charge of 100 soldiers) must have thought that Paul was just trying to get out of going to Rome. Now watch carefully and you will see a joyful faith:

> *When a gentle south wind began to blow, they saw their opportunity; so they weighed anchor and sailed along the shore of Crete. Before very long, a wind of hurricane force, called the Northeaster, swept down from the island. The ship was caught by the storm and could not head into the wind; so we gave way to it and were driven along. As we passed to the lee of a small island called Cauda, we were hardly able to make the lifeboat secure, so the men hoisted it aboard. Then they passed ropes under the ship itself to hold it together. Because they were afraid they would run aground on the sandbars of Syrtis, they lowered the sea anchor and let the ship be driven along. We took such a violent battering from the storm that the next day they began to throw the cargo overboard. On the third day, they threw the ship's tackle overboard with their own hands. When neither sun nor stars appeared for many days and the storm continued raging, we finally gave up all hope of being saved.*
>
> *After they had gone a long time without food, Paul stood up before them and said: "Men, you should have taken my advice not to sail from Crete; then you would have spared yourselves this damage and loss. But now I urge you to keep up your courage, because not one of you will be lost; only the ship will be destroyed. Last night an angel of the God to whom I belong and whom I serve stood beside me and said, 'Do not be afraid, Paul. You must stand trial before Caesar; and God has graciously given you the lives of all who sail with you.' So keep up your courage, men, for I have faith in God that it will happen just as he told me. Nevertheless, we must run aground on some island." (Acts 27:13–26)*

The storm hits. The cargo gets thrown overboard and there is much confusion. And then Paul says, "Cheer up!" Here is a deep joy in the midst of danger. Now, what was "seen"? A cheerful man on a sinking ship. Courage in the face of danger. Conviction in the face of doubt and real exhilaration in the place of sorrow. Paul had tremendous, refreshing joy when everyone else was scared out of their wits. That's joyful faith!

Now let's go back to the original question we were asking: what made Paul tick? We find the answer, again, in the book of Philippians: "*For to me, to live is Christ and to die is gain*" (Philippians 1:21).

Philosophers are always trying to find an answer to life and an answer to death. Paul's answer is this: While I live—Christ is always adequate. And when I die—Christ is still adequate. In fact, death is my gain. This must be the deep heart philosophy of any Christian.

When I really understand this deep in my inner being, then I am available to Christ. I am totally committed to him and thoroughly excited about him! What makes Paul tick even while in prison or in a shipwreck or being beaten? What's really going on at the center of his being? Now we can start to understand it. He is thinking that if he dies, it will be his gain. For Paul, life now is enjoying Jesus. And for Paul, heaven is enjoying Jesus without any disadvantages—no more shipwrecks, prisons, beatings, etc. If heaven is being with and enjoying Jesus, then I must enjoy Jesus now to be really excited about heaven. If I'm not excited now, why would I be excited later? Christ must be my life now!

Let's consider Paul with King Agrippa. There are just two possibilities for Paul. Possibility #1: "I will die." Possibility #2: "I will not die." So life is basically very simple—either live or die. To live is Christ. To die is gain. Paul knew he had already won either way!

Think about Paul on the sinking ship. Again, just two possibilities in his mind and heart. Possibility #1: "I'm going to drown." Possibility #2: "I'm not going to drown." Paul is thinking, "If I drown, I will die. If I don't drown, I will not die. If I go on living, then Christ is my life. If I die, death is my gain!"

Now go back to Paul being stoned and returning to finish his sermon. We know what's making him tick for sure now. He's thinking there are just two possibilities: "If they stone me, I will die. If they don't stone me, I live. If I die, death is my gain. If I live, Christ is my life. So go ahead if you must—throw those stones!"

Do you remember "super balls"? A super ball was a small, hard rubber ball that, when thrown on the ground, would bounce higher than you could imagine. Christians with joyful faith are like that super ball—the harder you throw them down, the higher they bounce back up! I have seen that in the life of my son, Kent. When Kent was in high school, he shared his faith with a girl in his class, inviting her to come to church. For some reason this girl's boyfriend got the wrong idea and in a jealous rage found Kent and then repeatedly punched him in the face. Kent was taken to the hospital with chipped teeth, deep bruises and a broken nose. Obviously, this was a very painful experience both emotionally and physically. Kent was struggling with what to do about this situation. The police wanted us to press charges. People in our lives were outraged and wanted some kind of payback. After input, talk and prayer we decided to invite the boy and his parents over to our house for a talk. During that time Kent told the boy that he forgave him and wanted to help him in any way he could. His whole family was amazed and incredibly grateful. As the years have passed, I don't know what happened to the other boy, but I do know how this shaped my son's life. He could have questioned God and gotten bitter. He could have become numb and uncaring towards others. He could have lost his faith at this critical moment. Instead he got hit hard but bounced back high. He developed a joyful faith: the harder you get hit, the higher you bounce back!

Shakespeare's play *Hamlet* has a famous line: "To be, or not to be." In context, Hamlet was saying that life is bad, and death will probably be worse. Now that's a bad situation. But with Paul, the answer to the question would simply be...YES. To go on being...Christ is his life. To not go on being...death is his gain. Christ must be this kind of reality in our lives! And, from personal experience, it's thrilling to have him as this kind of reality. He is all I need. He is bigger than any problem or challenge, bigger than any situation. And if this is what makes us tick, we will overcome any discouragement, fatigue or failure in our lives. We will live a victorious Christian life always remaining fully committed to God. Christ will be our life.

Questions: Is it tough to battle sin every day? Is it tough to be stared at and looked at funny when sharing your faith? Is it tough to deal with the time binds and pressures in life? We all answer these questions with a resounding YES, YES, YES! Well, here's the good news and the bad news: it's not going to get any easier in this life. Although the truth sounds bad, it's good to know this and accept it.

Let's turn our attention to Jesus for a moment:

> *. . . fixing our eyes on Jesus, the pioneer and perfecter of faith. For the joy set before him he endured the cross, scorning its shame, and sat down at the right hand of the throne of God. Consider him who endured such opposition from sinners, so that you will not grow weary and lose heart. (Hebrews 12:2–3)*

Jesus had joyful faith. Jesus is not only the *pioneer* of our faith; he is also the *perfecter* of our faith. We must learn from him just as Paul learned from him. When Jesus went through the most difficult and most challenging time of his life by going to the cross, it was because of *"the joy set before him"* that he was able to endure it. If you want to live like Jesus, then never let the crosses of life rob you of your joy. Don't think: the cross, the cross, the cross. You must think: the joy, the joy, the joy!

When the famous artist Renoir was old and crippled with arthritis, he would still get up every day to paint. After a period of time a concerned friend came and asked him, "Why do you put yourself through all the pain?" Renoir simply replied, "The pain passes, but the beauty remains." And that's how it is with faithful Christians. What we produce in our lives and in the lives of others will go on into eternity. The pain passes but the beauty remains!

So always remember Paul. Always remember Jesus. And always have a **JOYFUL FAITH**.

## PART FIVE

# LIVING FAITH

Years ago Kay and I were traveling by car from Florida to South Carolina. We stopped at a rest stop, got out, and then returned to the car and started driving again. A few miles down the road, Kay realized her engagement and wedding rings were missing. She had taken them off and put them on her lap before the rest stop. Now they were gone. We pulled over and started searching, hoping they were still in the car. After a few minutes we found both rings. At that point Kay's tears began to flow. She was so relieved and happy because something of both great sentimental value and great monetary value had been found.

When you lose something of value, you search until you find it. If someone came to you and said their child was missing, wouldn't you drop everything immediatley and help them search? And if someone told you they had lost their faith, or even some of their faith, wouldn't you stop to help them find it? If faith is valuable to you, you would. I hope that what you have read so far has been helping you find faith, understand faith and embrace faith in such a way that it will never be the same for you again. Our faith in God is what we should protect and prize the very most.

There are always people who are trying to hurt your faith in God. They want you to lose what is most precious to you. This happens in the form of arguments about the existence of God, about the resurrection of Jesus or about the truth of the Bible. Some say they only believe in what can be seen and scientifically proven. Anything else is just the work of an overactive imagination. And yet, people believe in love. It can't be seen although its effects can be seen. It can't be scientifically proven or measured but all the evidence says it exits! The resurrection can't be scientifically proven (repeated in the laboratory) but there is evidence to prove it's true. And the reality of the matter is that everyone who breathes lives by faith. Every time a person gets into a car and drives, they drive by faith. They have great faith in the brakes. Did they check them before driving down the road? And every time a person sits down, they sit by faith. Does anyone check to make sure the chair or stool will hold their weight? And so there is much faith in the chair. And on and on we could go with example after example. So anyone who says they do not live by any kind of faith is very out of touch!

But we are to live with faith in God. And without faith it is impossible to please God. Faith is an imperative because faith is the only way to begin and to sustain a relationship. Christianity, first and foremost, is all about having and maintaining a relationship with God. Without faith (trust and right actions), friendships cease. Without faith (trust and right actions), marriages die. Faith is what makes relationships possible. It is what makes our relationship with God possible. And God is worthy of our faith because he has proven his faithfulness to us by sending his Son to die for our sins. For all time, God shouts from the cross, "I love you!" He is always waiting for each individual to respond to his love with love. Faith is not an experiment; we must be totally committed to it. We must be willing to stake our lives on it. Living faith is faithful *until* death and faithful *unto* death!

After all, who is the true believer? If I asked any group of people if they believed a person could jump out of an airplane with a parachute and survive, go underwater with scuba gear for hours and survive or jump from a high bridge tied to a bungee cord and survive, everyone would say, "Absolutely yes." But if I asked who had ever been parachuting, had gone scuba diving or had done bungee jumping, there would only be a few hands going up in that same crowd. And these would be the few *true* believers because they were willing to put their lives on the line with what they believed. And when it comes to God, that's also the true believer or the one with living faith.

## Live Your Dream!

God wants you to live your faith or, to put it another way, *God wants you to live your dream!* But what is your dream? What are your *real* dreams in your life? We have already learned that God can do "*more than all we ask or imagine.*" God provides the power and the opportunities to live our dreams, but he does not make us use the power or use the opportunities. But know this: God doesn't want his children to just live life; he wants his children to live an amazing life! So what are your dreams? Are they about possessions or power or position? Are they about money and riches and security? God forbid that our great dreams are just worldly dreams in a spiritual wrapper. We must have godly dreams! Are you building and planning your life in such a way as to do extraordinary (extra-ordinary) things that glorify God? Are you taking your God-given talents, your God-given abilities, your God-given intellect, your God-given material wealth and your God-given profession and using them to accomplish God's will? Are you making a godly difference in this world at whatever age and stage you currently find yourself in?

All the questions above must be answered. And then the big question is: "What are you doing to make your dreams come true RIGHT NOW?" A recent book about publishing states that seventy-five percent of the U.S. population "dream" of being published and yet only two percent actually get published. This is just one illustration exposing the fact that most people spend their lives thinking or having good intentions to make their dreams come true *someday*...but that someday never comes. I have been in many conversations with people who are planning to do something big for God after they set their lives up financially, or after their kids are grown, or after they retire or...well, you get the idea. It never really happens. Living faith can't be "someday"; it has to be "today." So, what are you doing to make your dreams come true *right now*?

Dreaming is fun. Living your dream is more fun! In the play, *Les Miserables*, a song is sung entitled, "I Dreamed a Dream." The final line in the song is "Now life has killed the dream I dreamed." How tragic! Yet this is the basic pattern of life of most people as they age. People tend to stop dreaming in big and new ways. Let's look at the different stages of life and see some of the tendencies they display. Not everyone is exactly as will be described in the following life stages, but, as you will see, the pattern is generally true.

In the teen years, everything is a fight—a battle. Growing up is all about becoming your own person. Teens are idealistic. They want to make a difference with their lives and they believe they can. They challenge the status quo and ask, "Why not?" "Why not change the world?" Teens are looking for a purpose and a meaning to their existence. They want to be challenged; they are willing to take risks. And teens hate hypocrisy. God has placed inside teens the desire and need for something real and honest. When they see and experience hypocrisy, they rebel with a passion. They want truth. Teens are natural dreamers.

In the twenty-something years, people are looking for something to give their lives to—a focused purpose, a focused battle. During this time, people are moldable and unattached. This allows more time to be available for the pursuit of a dream. They are ready and willing to pour themselves out for a cause. They also want and desire challenges. They embrace being uncomfortable and being radical to accomplish lofty goals and dreams. At the same time, there is a tendency to be arrogant and prideful and disrespectful, thinking they know more and know better than those who have gone before them. They are looking for a lasting love and they believe it can be wonderful.

In the thirty-something years, the tendency is to start wanting more stability and comfort. People start to lose some of their ideals.

They have now lived long enough to feel some of the deep hurts, pains and disappointments that come in life. They tend to resist the big and radical challenges. The attitude of "I've heard all this before" starts to creep in and starts to insidiously destroy their ability to dream big dreams.

In the forty-something and fifty-something years, there is a growing desire for more security—especially financial security. It is the time of the midlife crisis (sports cars and motorcycles and trophy wives!). People start to say to themselves, "Is this it?" "Is this all there is to my life?" "Is this all I am or will ever accomplish in my life?" They start to keenly feel the monotony of their lives or their work, and the monotony of their relationships. They start to question themselves: "Do I want to do the same thing I've been doing, for the rest of my life?" "Am I really happy?" "Am I fulfilled?" "Am I satisfied?" "Must I settle for just this?" They can feel miserable, to some extent because they don't see themselves changing and becoming more. In some ways they have given up and given in. There is a settling in and a settling for so much less than what they thought life would be. People at this age can start looking down on the enthusiasm and the idealism of youth. They have now tasted enough failure, hurt and pain to become cynical and disinterested to some degree. They can tend to distance themselves from being concerned, caring and involved. It is a time where many either break out of their marriage, their family and their job—or they may become even more passionate and committed to their jobs and profession in the midst of failed marriages and failed families. They are seeking to feel good about themselves. The tendency, more than ever, is to go for all the material comforts and pleasures before being too old (or dead) to enjoy them.

And then in their sixties, seventies and eighties people are becoming more and more health conscious. The subject of health can dominate almost every conversation. At this age, people are in touch as never before with their own mortality, as friends and loved ones are dying. Many grow bitter and angry with life. Most have broken relationships that leave them lonely and afraid. Some just exist through the rest of their days as they live with their regrets, guilt and shame from the bad choices made in their lives. To cover up and not really deal with the regrets, guilt and shame, they start to speak in terms of the "glory days"—how good things were in earlier years. Often, it is an imaginary past reality to make the present reality more bearable.

As I have said, not everyone is exactly like this, but this is a recognized general pattern of aging. But with faith in God, the stages of life can be different. Faith can help us overcome our human challenges, tendencies, weaknesses and sins as we go through life. We all get older; we all age, but living faith works in our lives so that we don't have to be molded into the pattern of this world. We can keep growing and keep becoming all we were created to be! We can keep a spiritual life with a spiritual and positive perspective through all the stages of life.

Living faith is needed for all seasons of life. As we mentioned in Faith Secret 8, there are seasons of joy and seasons of sorrow. There is the season of dating, the season of marriage, the seasons of child bearing and child raising. There are the seasons of financial blessings and the seasons of financial challenges. There are the seasons of health issues; the seasons of church issues; the seasons of job issues; the seasons of stress, loneliness and faith struggles. And, finally, there will be the season of our own death. Jesus has the answers and the needed encouragement. He has the direction, help, comfort, hope and inspiration everyone needs in this life. Living faith is what we were created to experience.

We are all dreamers, because God made us like that. Yet most of us let go of our dreams somewhere in life. When we do, we die inside and become the walking dead. Some dreams that we have for ourselves are unrealistic. As a kid I dreamed of being a rock star, a pro football player and a movie star. These were not realistic for me, considering I can't sing, am not a great athlete and don't do well with memorizing lines. Later, some of my dreams were to become a lawyer, write books and live on an island in a warm climate. Some dreams that may actually be attainable are put aside when we decide to follow Jesus. God lets us choose so many dreams: We get to choose our profession (for me, I have my dream job preaching and teaching). We get to choose our spouse (I married my dream girl). And God allows us to choose the dreams of where to live, things to do, places to see and experiences to be enjoyed. But God also has dreams we are to adopt and make our own when we say "Jesus is Lord." This would include the dream of living a pure life, the dream of having a loving marriage, the dream of having spiritual families and the dream of an evangelized world. To adopt God's dreams for our lives we *always* have to radically reshape, rethink, replan and reorganize our lives in both big and little ways. We call this repentance—turning our lives around 180 degrees as we surrender everything to God. And then we have to make sure we keep turned around and keep surrendered. As we do that, we will need to make continual adjustments so that we stay on track. It's like driving. We can be headed in the right direction, but we have to keep adjusting the wheel to stay on the road.

Certainly, it is a challenge to keep dreaming for God. At different points in our lives we find we have accomplished certain dreams. At other points in our lives we find that certain dreams have been smashed either through time, sin or circumstance. What we must do is continually revive and replace our dreams as we go through life. Your only limitation is the size of your faith. When you have big faith, think big thoughts, make big plans, then God will bless you with big results. Don't ever believe the lie that says you can't when God says you can! The Bible still contains the words: "*I can do everything through Christ who gives me strength*" (Philippians 4:13). And those words are eternally true!

**Why not take some time today to start making your bucket list? These are the things you will do in your life before you die, or "kick the bucket." List your top 100 dream things to accomplish, see, experience and enjoy. Make sure you have great kingdom dreams incorporated in your list. Then start living your dreams!**

## The Will of God

To have a living faith, we must seek to know God's will and then be willing to do his will. It's a choice: *"Anyone who **chooses** to do the **will of God** will find out whether my teaching comes from God or whether I speak on my own"* (John 7:17, emphasis added).

We make the big choice when we initially say "Jesus is Lord" at the time we are baptized into Christ for the forgiveness of sins. What a huge difference that makes in how a person lives life! Everything changes when we are done with the practice of sin. And we are so happy to no longer be living in the muck and mire of it. Our attitude is not, "Gee whiz, I don't get to live like that anymore." Instead it's, "Thank God I don't have to live like that anymore!"

> *Therefore, since Christ suffered in his body, arm yourselves also with the same attitude, because whoever suffers in the body is done with sin. As a result, they do not live the rest of their earthly lives for evil human desires, but rather for the **will of God**. For you have spent enough time in the past doing what pagans choose to do — living in debauchery, lust, drunkenness, orgies, carousing and detestable idolatry. (1 Peter 4:1–3, emphasis added)*

That choice that we make every day to live in the will of God is not one we have to do alone. We have a spiritual family to be a part of.

> *Then Jesus' mother and brothers arrived. Standing outside, they sent someone in to call him. A crowd was sitting around him, and they told him, "Your mother and brothers are outside looking for you."*

> *"Who are my mother and my brothers?" he asked.*
>
> *Then he looked at those seated in a circle around him and said, "Here are my mother and my brothers! Whoever does **God's will** is my brother and sister and mother." (Mark 3:31–35, emphasis added)*

God's will is something we must desire, search out and decide to do throughout our Christian lives. It's not a one-time thing; it's an ongoing thing. It is because of the grace of God that we are motivated to be totally committed to having a living faith.

> *Therefore, I urge you, brothers and sisters, in view of God's mercy, to offer your bodies as a living sacrifice, holy and pleasing to God — this is your true and proper worship. Do not conform to the pattern of this world, but be transformed by the renewing of your mind. Then you will be able to test and approve what **God's will** is — his good, pleasing and perfect will. (Romans 12:1–2, emphasis added)*

At the end of our lives, only one thing will matter: did I keep choosing and living the will of God?

> *You need to persevere so that when you have done the **will of God**, you will receive what he has promised. (Hebrews 10:36, emphasis added)*

> *The world and its desires pass away, but whoever does the **will of God** lives forever. (1 John 2:17, emphasis added)*

The sacrifices and big decisions to do God's will are necessary throughout life. The biggest challenges come from the busyness of life, the desire to make money and being overly consumed with moving up the education, corporate, military or government ladder. For example, in making a move from one place to another, many are more driven by the worldly opportunity instead of being driven by their faith. It's like the old story of the preacher who was offered a better financial opportunity in a place he would rather live. He came home and said to his wife, "Honey, I'm going to go upstairs and pray about this decision, and you start packing!"

Let's *really* look at the passage in James 4. This is yet another passage that talks about the will of God:

> *Now listen, you who say, "Today or tomorrow we will go to this or that city, spend a year there, carry on business and make money." Why, you do not even know what will happen tomorrow. What is your life? You are a mist that appears for a little while and then vanishes. Instead, you ought to say, "If it is* ***the Lord's will,*** *we will live and do this or that." As it is, you boast in your arrogant schemes. All such boasting is evil. If anyone, then, knows the good they ought to do and doesn't do it, it is sin for them. (James 4:13–17, emphasis added)*

In this passage James is talking to Christians who do not have a living faith. They are making life decisions based on making money and are conveniently forgetting about eternity. They are forgetting that they are but a mist that will vanish. James gives us explicit direction on how to have a living faith. A person ought to first ask the question, "Is it the Lord's will?" before making any decision. When we choose our will over God's will, we are told it is arrogant and boastful and evil. When a person fails to do the good they ought to do (fails to choose God's will) then for them, it is sin.

So how does a person make a spiritual decision instead of a worldly one? How does a person choose God's will? Here's a good process:

1. Ask yourself: What is God's will?
2. Go to God in prayer.
3. Search the Bible. What does the Bible say specifically or in principle about the decision you are making?
4. Go to God in prayer.
5. Ask for spiritual advice from spiritual people (Proverbs 12:15; Proverbs 19:20; Proverbs 20:18). Don't go to the one you know will give you the answer you want to hear!
6. Go to God in prayer.

7. Make the decision that is in agreement with God's will. There may be more than one option that is in the will of God.
8. When you don't get the answer you wanted and you still desire to do what you know is not God's will, go to your own Gethsemane and seek to become surrendered. You need to do what Jesus did. Spend time with God until you can say as Jesus said, *"Not what I will, but what you will."*

We have to ask ourselves some tough questions! Is it my will or is it God's will? Am I just putting some spiritual language or spin on the decision I want? Will this help or hurt the spirituality of my family? Will this allow me to have a greater or lesser impact in God's kingdom? This all has to do with having living faith, faith that is alive, faith that is being lived out in everyday life. God wants us to be happy and to enjoy life. We have to believe that living in the parameters of his will is the only way to have a great life. After all, it is totally futile to try and live a great life without a great relationship with God. And the only way to have a great relationship with God is to be living in the will of God.

In John 4:34, Jesus says, "*My food...is to do the will of the one who sent me and to finish his work.*" I don't know about you, but I like food. Food is fun. It makes you grow; it keeps you healthy and energizes you. Food fills you up. I need food to live. In the same way, I need the will of God to be filled up and satisfied, to enjoy life and to even survive!

## An "Even-If" Faith

To have living faith, you have to have *even-if faith*. This is another way of saying tested faith. The testing of our faith strengthens it and makes it genuine. The testing of our faith is what matures us and completes us. It's not that we enjoy the trial itself, but we enjoy what the trial produces in our lives and in our faith.

*Consider it pure joy, my brothers and sisters, whenever you face trials of many kinds, because you know that the testing of your faith produces perseverance. Let perseverance finish its work so that you may be mature and complete, not lacking anything. (James 1:2–4)*

I am in awe every time I consider the faith of Abraham with his willingness to sacrifice his son, Isaac. When he got the command to do this, he did not hesitate. He got up early the next day to leave for the sacrifice. The only way he could even consider taking the life of his own son was to have the faith that God could raise him from the dead. As you know, God did not literally let the son die. He was setting up the premise for the salvation of mankind by demonstrating the ability to have a substitutionary sacrifice or substitutionary death. Jesus would become our substitutionary sacrifice so that we could be set free. So Abraham had an even-if faith: *even if* my son dies, I will obey my God.

*By faith Abraham, when God tested him, offered Isaac as a sacrifice. He who had embraced the promises was about to sacrifice his one and only son, even though God had said to him, "It is through Isaac that your offspring will be reckoned." Abraham reasoned that God could even raise the dead, and so in a manner of speaking he did receive Isaac back from death. (Hebrews 11:17–19)*

Do you have an even-if kind of faith? Shadrach, Meshach and Abednego did. They believed God could save them but *even if* God chose not to save them, they would only bow down and worship the one true God.

*"If we are thrown into the blazing furnace, the God we serve is able to deliver us from it, and he will deliver us from Your Majesty's hand. But even if he does not, we want you to know, Your Majesty, that we will not serve your gods or worship the image of gold you have set up." (Daniel 3:17–18)*

Esther had even-if faith. By coming before the king without being summoned, she knew she could lose her life. But this is what she had to do to save the Jews from extinction. She had faith in God and was willing to do the heroic thing *even if* God allowed her to die.

> *"Go, gather together all the Jews who are in Susa, and fast for me. Do not eat or drink for three days, night or day. I and my attendants will fast as you do. When this is done, I will go to the king, even though it is against the law. And* ***if*** *I perish, I perish." (Esther 4:16,)*

Job was another person who had great even-if faith. At times the people who should be most on our side or our best cheerleaders are not there for us. But our faith cannot be dependent on having the support of others. And our faith has to stand firm in the midst of the many "unfair" and unexpected events that occur in life. The death of a child. The loss of job, income or house. The news of bad health. Job struggled as we all would, but he struggled to victory.

> *His wife said to him, "Are you still maintaining your integrity? Curse God and die!"*
>
> *He replied, "You are talking like a foolish woman. Shall we accept good from God, and not trouble?"*
>
> *In all this, Job did not sin in what he said. (Job 2:9–10)*

Habakkuk expressed an even-if faith in a beautiful and poetic way. *Even if* he couldn't see the blessings at the moment, he found joy in his relationship with God. Delayed blessings are often the test of the strength of a person's faith.

> *Though the fig tree does not bud*
> *and there are no grapes on the vines,*
> *though the olive crop fails*
> *and the fields produce no food,*
> *though there are no sheep in the pen*
> *and no cattle in the stalls,*
> *yet I will rejoice in the LORD,*
> *I will be joyful in God my Savior.*
> *The Sovereign LORD is my strength;*
> *he makes my feet like the feet of a deer,*
> *he enables me to tread on the heights. (Habakkuk 3:17–19)*

## The Ultimate Dream—The Ultimate Price

Living faith is faith that is willing to die for the cause of Jesus Christ. The apostle John tells us we are to be faithful to the point of death! (Revelation 2:10). If this is not a reality in our hearts, then neither is living faith a reality in our hearts. Although it can only be true for most of us in theory, it is to be the solid decision we must have already made in our hearts and minds because we are actual followers of Jesus.

The ultimate dream is to be with God in eternity. Imagine if you could interview a baby in his mother's womb. You ask, "Do you believe in life after birth?" The unborn child answers: "Well, now, I don't know. It seems scary because I've never experienced it. I'd probably rather just stay in the womb, where it's warm and comfortable and I can enjoy all the food I want. And I even get to go swimming every day!" The interview abruptly ends because all of a sudden, the baby is born. He enters into the light and into a place so much greater and bigger than anything he could ever have imagined. He meets his parents, who are overjoyed to hold him in their arms. Yes, there is life after birth. And yes, there is life after death!

Now, let me repeat, we are called to be faithful (full of faith) even to the point of death. Paul had that kind of living faith.

> *"I am ready not only to be bound, but also to die in Jerusalem for the name of the Lord Jesus" (Acts 21:13).*

> *For to me, to live is Christ and to die is gain (Philippians 1:21).*

The truth is that we don't really believe in something until we are willing to stake our lives on it. Being willing to give our money, our time and our effort demonstrates a commitment. Being willing to die demonstrates a total commitment; it demonstrates a living faith. Consider the following:

**Jesus**, Son of God – beaten, whipped, crucified on a cross in Jerusalem
**James**, son of Zebedee – AD 44, beheaded
**Philip** – preached the gospel in upper Asia; scourged, imprisoned, crucified, AD 54
**Matthew** – preached the gospel in Parthia, Ethiopia; slain with a halberd in AD 60
**Matthias** – stoned at Jerusalem and then beheaded
**Andrew** – preached in Asiatic nations; crucified on a cross
**Peter** – crucified upside down
**Thaddeus** – crucified in AD 72
**Bartholomew** – much work in India; beaten and crucified there
**Thomas** – preached in Parthia and India; thrust through with a spear
**Simon** the Zealot – preached in Africa and Britain; crucified AD 74
**Paul** – beheaded in Rome

There is a legend about a group of worshippers in the first century who gathered on a Sunday morning. As they were about to begin, a Roman soldier suddenly kicked open the door and, with sword in hand, demanded that they stop immediately. He said that anyone who wanted to leave could do so. They just needed to say the words, "Caesar is Lord." If they refused, they would die. After a few moments, a number of them said the required words and went out the door. The soldier proceeded to kick the door closed, put down his sword and say, "Yes, you will all die...*someday*. But today, let's have a great time of worship together. I just wanted to be with the *real* Christians this morning!"

To make it to heaven it will take a living faith. It will take a living faith to enjoy life, to make an impact for Christ and to have spiritual marriages and families. To evangelize the world it will take a living faith.

## A Final Thought

As I close out this book on radical faith, I want to say that faith cannot be simply put in a box (or in a book) with a beautiful bow tied around it and a card saying, "Here it is; come and get it!" There is still much mystery concerning faith, and I believe God wants it just that way. Being somewhat mysterious makes it quite attractive! Faith is one of those things wrapped in the infinite and we, who are trying to understand it, are only finite. Still, God has given us much we *can* understand, *can* learn and *can* embrace in our lives about faith. I hope these 10 Faith Secrets have opened your mind, your emotions and your imagination to a greater appreciation and a greater understanding of faith. I pray it will make a RADICAL difference in how you live your life for God. I also pray it will make a RADICAL difference in what you accomplish in your life for God. After all, that's what happens when you have RADICAL FAITH!

I will leave you with this story...

There was once a man who was climbing a tall mountain alone. He had a heavy backpack on and was soon to be at the top. As he was making his final ascent to the summit, he lost his footing and began falling and sliding down towards a 1000-foot cliff. At the last moment he grabbed on by his finger tips and was holding on for dear life. He was now hanging seemingly in midair. With his backpack on he couldn't lift himself up and if he let go with one hand to try to drop the backpack he wouldn't be able to hold on. So he did the only thing he could do. He yelled for help.

"PLEASE HELP ME! HELP! HELP! HELP!"

No one came. No one answered. And so he yelled to God. "PLEASE HELP ME, GOD! I'LL DO ANYTHING! HELP ME, GOD!"

And then a little angel sent from God appeared. And he said to the mountain climber, "So you'll do *anything*?"

The man was now losing his strength to hold on and

screamed, "YES...I'LL DO *ANYTHING!*"

The angel in a soft, gentle voice said, "Alright. No problem. Just let go and...I'll catch you."

God says the same thing to us: just let go and I'll catch you. God has great plans for your life. He wants you to experience success and desires you to victoriously live the life you were created to live. Just let go of whatever is holding you back from doing all the great things I know you want to do with your life for God. Have faith that God will always catch you. You'll be amazed at what happens. Just let go, and let God!

## Also available from www.ipibooks.com

Our Beginnings

*Genesis Through the Eyes of A Woman*

by Kay Summers McKean

Price: $11.99

## Also available from www.ipibooks.com

Love Your Husband

by Gloria Baird and Kay Summers McKean

Price: $11.99

Also available from www.ipibooks.com

A Women's Ministry Handbook

by Jennifer Lambert and Kay Summers McKean

Price: $12.99

www.ipibooks.com